History of the Town of
SMITHFIELD

From
Its Organization in 1730-31
to
Its Division in 1871

Compiled in Accordance with the Votes of the
Towns of Smithfield, North Smithfield,
Lincoln, and Woonsocket,
Rhode Island

Thomas Steere

HERITAGE BOOKS
2016

HERITAGE BOOKS

AN IMPRINT OF HERITAGE BOOKS, INC.

Books, CDs, and more—Worldwide

For our listing of thousands of titles see our website
at
www.HeritageBooks.com

A Facsimile Reprint
Published 2016 by
HERITAGE BOOKS, INC.
Publishing Division
5810 Ruatan Street
Berwyn Heights, Md. 20740

International Standard Book Numbers
Paperbound: 978-1-55613-655-9
Clothbound: 978-0-7884-6483-6

NOTE.

The undersigned desires to express his obligations to the Hon. Joshua M. Addeman, Hon. Samuel Clark, the late Hon. Charles Moies, and the late Thomas A. Paine, for valuable aid in the prosecution of his work. He is indebted to Erastus Richardson's History of Woonsocket for suggestions and the smoothing the path of investigation.

The death of the Hon. Charles Moies and Thomas A. Paine, members of the town committees during the progress of the duty accepted by the writer, has removed from Lincoln and Woonsocket men of pronounced ability and character, who have left no survivors more embued with Rhode Island sentiment and conservatism, or more faithful in the performance of public trusts than themselves. As they were representative men in Old Smithfield, so were their acts and example such as to stimulate and encourage public spirit, public honesty and genuine patriotism.

THOMAS STEERE.

PUBLIC RESOLUTION

Passed by Congress and Approved by the President, March 13th, 1876.

———————

JOINT RESOLUTION on the celebration of the Centennial in the several counties and towns.

Be it resolved by the Senate and House of Representatives of the United States of America in Congress assembled, That it be, and is hereby recommended by the Senate and House of Representatives to the people of the several States that they assemble in their several counties or towns on the approaching centennial anniversary of our national independence, and that they cause to have delivered on such day an historical sketch of said county or town from its formation, and that a copy of said sketch may be filed, in print or manuscript, in the clerk's office of said county, and an additional copy, in print or manuscript, be filed in the office of the librarian of congress, to the intent that a complete record may thus be obtained of the progress of our institutions during the first centennial of their existence.

PRESIDENT'S PROCLAMATION.

By the President of the United States.

A PROCLAMATION.

Whereas, A joint resolution of the Senate and House of Representatives of the United States was duly approved on the 13th day of March last, which resolution is as follows:

"Be it resolved by the Senate and House of Representatives of the United States of America in Congress assembled, that it be and is hereby recommended by the Senate and the House of Representatives to the people of the several States that they assemble in their several counties or towns on the approaching centennial anniversary of our national independence, and that they cause to have delivered on such day an historical sketch of said county or town from its formation, and that a copy of said sketch may be filed in print or manuscript, in the clerk's office of said county, and an additional copy in print or manuscript be filed in the office of the librarian of Congress, to the intent that a complete record may thus be obtained of the progress of our institutions during the first centennial of their existence"; and

Whereas, It is deemed proper that such recommendation be brought to the notice and knowledge of the people of the United States,

Now, therefore, I, Ulysses S. Grant, President of the United States, do hereby declare and make known the same, in the hope that the object of such resolution may meet the approval of the people of the United States, and that proper steps may be taken to carry the same into effect.

Given under my hand, at the city of Washington, the 25th day of May, in the year of our Lord 1876, and of the independence of the United States the one hundredth.

By the President,   U. S. GRANT.

Hamilton Fish, Secretary of State.

State of Rhode Island, &c.

In General Assembly, January Session, A. D, 1876.

JOINT RESOLUTION ON THE CELEBRATION OF THE CENTENNIAL IN THE SEVERAL CITIES AND TOWNS.

Resolved, The House of Representatives concurring therein, that in accordance with the recommendation of the National Congress, the Governor be requested to invite the people of the several cities and towns of the State, to assemble in their several localities on the approaching Centennial Anniversary of our National Independence, and cause to have delivered on that day an historical sketch of said town or city from its formation, and to have one copy of said sketch, in print or manuscript, filed in the clerk's office of said town or city, one copy in the office of the Secretary of State, and one copy in the office of the librarian of Congress, to the intent that a complete record may thus be obtained of the progress of our institutions during the first centennial of their existence; and that the Governor be requested to communicate the invitation forthwith to the several town and city councils in the State.

I certify the foregoing to be a true copy of a resolution passed by the General Assembly of the State aforesaid, on the 20th day of April, A. D. 1876.

Witness my hand and Seal of the State, this 27th day of April, A. D. 1876.

{ L. S. }

JOSHUA M. ADDEMAN,
Secretary of State.

B

State of Rhode Island, &c.

EXECUTIVE DEPARTMENT,
PROVIDENCE, April 27th, 1876.

To the Honorable Town Council of the Town of ————.

GENTLEMEN:—I have the honor to enclose a duly certified copy of a resolution passed by the General Assembly, at its recent session, requesting me to invite the people of the several towns and cities of the State, to assemble in their several localities on the approaching Centennial Anniversary of our National Independence, and cause to have delivered on such day an historical sketch of said town or city from its formation.

By pursuing the course suggested by the resolution of the General Assembly, the people of the State will derive an amount of information which will be invaluable to the present generation, as showing the wonderful progress of the several towns and cities since their foundation.

It will also be of great value to future generations when the materials for such sketches now accessible will have been lost or destroyed by accident, or become more or less effaced and illegible from time. Therefore, in pursuance of the request of the General Assembly, I respectfully and earnestly, through you, invite the people of your town to carry out the contemplated celebration on the fourth day of July next.

HENRY LIPPITT, Governor.

LINCOLN.

At a Town Meeting held in Lincoln, on the thirteenth day of June, A. D. 1876, it was

Voted, That we hereby recommend and advise that the Town Council, in accordance with the contemplated action of the General Assembly, take necessary action in the matter of making the written history of the old Town of Smithfield, and printing the same, of which the Town of Lincoln was formerly a part thereof, and that the said Town Council be authorized to expend not more than Five Hundred dollars in defraying the expense thereof; the whole cost of said history to be borne by the towns of Smithfield, North Smithfield and Lincoln, and the sum above appropriated is that the town of Lincoln may pay towards the whole cost of said history in proportion to its payment of the old Town of Smithfield's indebtedness at the time of the division of the old Town of Smithfield in 1871.

WOONSOCKET.

At a Town Council holden within and for the town of Woonsocket, June 15th, 1876, Thomas A. Paine was "appointed a committee to confer with committees appointed by other towns regarding the preparation of a history of the old town of Smithfield."

July 10th, a verbal report was made recommending that this Council make an appropriation for the purpose of the history; whereupon the whole matter was referred to Dr. Ariel Ballou, Spencer Mowry, Thomas A. Paine, Charles Nourse and Darius D. Farnum as a committee to consider the subject and make recommendations to the Council as soon as may be. On August 1st, 1876, "The committee heretofore appointed by this Council to consider and recommend suitable action on the subject matter of aiding in the publication of a history of the old town of Smithfield, make report in writing recommending that a committee of one be appointed to confer with the committees appointed by the respective towns of Lincoln, Smithfield and North Smithfield having this matter in charge, also recommending that a sum of money not exceeding one hundred dollars be appropriated to pay the attendant expenses; also recommending that Thomas A. Paine, Esq., be appointed as such committee;" whereupon said report is received and ordered placed on file, and it is

Voted, That the recommendations contained in said report be adopted, and Thomas A. Paine is hereby appointed as such committee, and the sum of one hundred dollars is appropriated for the purpose aforesaid.

SMITHFIELD.

At a Town Council held at the Hotel in Greenville, within and for the Town of Smithfield, on Saturday, June 24, 1876, present John S. Appleby, Thurston E. Phetteplace, Henry E. Smith, Edwin C. Harris and William Gardiner, members of said Council;

Voted, That the sum of Two Hundred (200) Dollars be and the same is hereby appropriated to defray the expense incurred in connection with the towns of Lincoln and North Smithfield, in compiling and publishing the history of the old town of Smithfield; and that Samuel W. Farnum be and he is hereby appointed a committee on the part of the present town of Smithfield to assist in the compilation of said work.

Witness:
         M. I. MOWRY,
          Deputy Town Clerk.

At a Town Council held at the Justice Court Room in Georgiaville, within and for the Town of Smithfield, on Friday the first day of December, A. D. 1876, present John S. Appleby, president, and Henry E. Smith, William Gardiner and Edwin C. Harris, members of said Council, Arlon Mowry, Esq., committee of the town of North Smithfield, for compiling and publishing a Historical Sketch of the old Town of Smithfield, appeared in behalf of said North Smithfield and the towns of Lincoln and Woonsocket, and requested this Council to appoint a committee to act in conjunction with the committees of said towns of North Smithfield, Lincoln and Woonsocket in compiling and publishing said Historical Sketch; stating that the joint committee of the several towns proposed to assume the payment of the One Hundred and Fifty Dollars already paid Hon. Samuel W. Farnum by this town for writing a Historical Sketch of said old Smithfield, and that the said joint committee would consider the said sketch prepared by said Samuel W. Farnum as the property of said committee, and would make such disposition of the same as their judgment should determine; and upon consideration of said matter, it was voted that Jabez W. Mowry be appointed a committee for the purpose aforesaid, with authority to act, as such committee, in such manner as he shall deem expedient and proper.

Witness:
       OSCAR A. TOBEY,
        Council Clerk.

NORTH SMITHFIELD.

Voted, That we hereby recommend and advise that the Town Council of this Town, in accordance with the contemplated act of the General Assembly, take necessary action in the matter of making the written history of the old town of Smithfield, and printing the same, of which the town of North Smithfield was formerly a part thereof, and that said Town Council be authorized to expend not more than four hundred dollars in defraying the expense thereof, the whole cost of said history is to be borne conjointly by the towns of Smithfield, North Smithfield and Lincoln, and the sum above appropriated is that this town may pay towards the total cost of said history in proportion to the old town debt.

Voted, That Arlon Mowry, Esq., be a committee to attend to the carrying out the aforegoing vote.

CHAPTER I.

THE town of Smithfield was originally a portion of the territory of the town of Providence. The town of Providence was settled by Roger Williams and the men who accompanied him from Plymouth Colony. As Roger Williams gave to Providence its social and political spirit, and impressed upon it a character still distinct and dominant; and inasmuch as the first settlers of the town of Smithfield were men who moved from, and were imbued with the principles underlying the government of Providence, we shall only obtain a clear understanding of their views and purposes by a glance at the rise and history of Providence up to the time that Smithfield was set off therefrom; and we shall only comprehend the history of Providence by an intelligent conception of the man by whom it was founded. The starting point, then, of the history of Smithfield, is an enquiry as to who and what was Roger Williams.

Roger Williams, according to the best authorities was born in Wales, near the close of the sixteenth century. He was elected a scholar of the Charter-House, June 25, 1621; and was matriculated a pensioner of Pembroke College, Cambridge, July 7, 1625. He took the degree of Bachelor of Arts, January, 1627. He sailed from Bristol, England, with his wife Mary, in the ship Lyon, December 1, 1630, and after a voyage of sixty-six days, arrived off Nantasket, February 5, 1631. This man, in the very flush of early

manhood, who had been educated in the learning of the
schools, who had so well improved his opportunities as to
receive the friendship and esteem of the wisest and best in
England, and the confidence and companionship of the ablest
in the colonies, was soon invited to become teacher of the
Boston Church, which proposition he declined because he
"durst not officiate to an unseparated people." Without
stopping to discuss ecclesiastical doctrines or forms, it is
noticeable that the very first moment in which Roger Williams relates himself, or is called upon to connect himself
especially and responsibly to the people, he makes his conduct a point of conscience. In itself the offered pastorship
might well enough have been undertaken by Roger Williams, but his scruples would not permit him to endorse
what he thought to be a deficient evidence of faith, even
by implication.

In April, 1631, he was invited to the church at Salem,
but the authorities interfered, and during the summer he
went to Plymouth, where he became assistant to Ralph Smith.
Here again, and so soon his restless mind and teasing conscience urged him to compose a "treatise" against the
Patent, which brought him into collision with the magistrates, but upon submission, he was relieved from the threatened censure. Before the close of 1633, he returned to
Salem, assisting the Rev. Mr. Skelton, but "in not any
office." In August, 1634, after the death of Skelton, he
was called to be teacher to the church. In November,
1634, he was summoned before the Court for having broken
his promise "in teaching publicly against the King's patent."
But at the March session, proceedings were again suspended,
on the ground that his action sprang from "exemplary conscience rather than seditious principle." When the Court
met again, April 30, a new charge was brought against him
of withstanding the Freeman's oath. Early in the summer
of 1635, the Salem Church proceeded with his ordination,

which led to his being cited before the Court, July 8, on the ground that "being under question for divers dangerous opinions" he had been called "in contempt of authority" to the office of teacher. At the October session of the Court, sentence was passed upon him, requiring him "to depart out of this jurisdiction within six weeks." Being seized soon after with a serious illness, he was permitted to remain till spring, but as he persisted in maintaining and promulgating his opinions, it was decided in January, 1636, to send him to England. He fled to the forest. For fourteen weeks he wandered in the woods "not knowing what bread or bed did mean." In the spring of 1636, he began to "build and plant" at Seekonk, but in June, in consequence of a friendly intimation from the authorities of Plymouth that he had settled within their bounds, set about finding, as he hoped, a permanent abiding place. In June, looking across the Seekonk river, he saw a pleasant land crowned with noble trees just bursting into luxuriant foliage. The waters northward were attractive in their placid beauty. Behind was one irate colony, and another inhospitable; before him was the Indian, whom he knew, and no white man to disturb, or be disturbed. Hitherto, however one may partition the indiscretions or the wrongs, Roger Williams had found in America neither peace, nor the opportunity for doing good. If, as must be confessed, he was legally wrong in impugning the validity of the Massachusetts patent, it was because of a principle which he honestly and fully carried out when his time and temptation came. The Great and General Court of Massachusetts had exercised its authority; Plymouth had warned him away; how would the red man receive him as one who came among them to stay. The future was as impenetrable as the forest at midnight. One could only predict that whatever might come to pass Roger Williams would be Roger Williams still.

And here it is proper to ask in what spirit, and for what

purpose Roger Williams came into this then wilderness where only one white man, William Blackstone, had preceded him in 1635, and who had settled at Study Hill, within the limits of the Plymouth Colony, now Cumberland, and on the banks of the Pawtucket, now called Blackstone river. It was no worldly ambition which impelled Williams forward; nor was it a simple desire for a peaceful and inactive life. No idea had entered his mind of forming a State. The five companions whom he permitted to cross the Seekonk with him in his canoe, he brought at their request and from motives of compassion. His purpose was to preach to the Indians. In his own expressive language: " My soul's desire was to do the natives good." He was well educated; he had seen the power exercised by, and the great deference paid to the leaders in the colony of Massachusetts Bay; in learning he was their equal; in ability to gain the friendship of, and deal with the natives their superior, but he sought no personal aggrandizement, he was in heart and in intent a missionary to the heathen. And we may readily accept his own interpretation of his aims because his whole life bore out and exemplified the professions he made.

Nor did he come unprepared for his work. He had already studied with equal diligence and effect the language of the natives; he had "lodged with them in their filthy smoky holes;" he had learned their ways, and had disciplined himself to bear with, and by kindness to control them. Moreover, as he had conscientiously written against the King's patent in Massachusetts, so here he honestly acknowledged the rights of the aborigines, and procured of them the titles to the land he wished to acquire. He bought of the Indians, but not alone by presents or commercial purchase. " It was not," he says, " thousands, nor tens of thousands of money that could have bought an English entrance into this bay, but I was the procurer of the purchase by that language, acquaintance and favor with the natives, and other advantages, which it pleased God to give me." The land was deeded to Williams by Canonicus and Miantonomi, and was his own individual property "as much as any man's coat on his back." But desiring to make his purchase "a shelter for persons distressed for conscience," he "communicated his purchase unto his loving friends." Now he has included in his benevolent purposes others besides the Indians, deeds an equal share with himself to twelve who were his companions, "and such others as the major part shall admit into the same fellowship of vote." And so was formed a Commonwealth in "the unmixed form of a pure democracy."

The first written compact so far as is now known, was in these words: "We whose names are hereunder, desirous to inhabit in the town of Providence, do promise to subject ourselves in active or passive obedience to all such orders or agreements as shall be made for public good of the body, in an orderly way, by the major assent of the present inhabitants, masters of families, incorporated together into a town fellowship, and such others whom they shall admit unto them, only in civil things." Such was the foundation, not only of a "lively experiment" in government, but of a community in which the line of demarcation between the temporal and spiritual power was for the first time in the history of the world definitely and emphatically drawn. Obedience to the political authority, in a word to the government was to be, and only to be "in civil things." The doctrine of these men was not toleration, but liberty in religious belief. Law, Order, Liberty of Conscience. Upon this basis was the government of Providence founded. And to-day the spirit of this band of pioneers rests upon and actuates the citizens of Rhode Island. The statute book, the tone and temper of the people, the institutions, the peculiarities of our several local communities bear witness as well to the vividness as to the strength of this theory of government.

And under this plain compact, and under a King's Charter, and under a written Constitution, ever and alike the democracy and the religious liberty of the Commonwealth have been maintained.

The earliest conveyance of land, to be found in the records of Providence, is in these words:

" At Nanhiggansick the 24th of the first month commonly called March, in the second year of our plantation or planting at Mooshausick or Providence.   Memorandum, that we Cannannicus and Meauntonomi, the two chief sachems of Nanhiggansick, having two years since sold unto Roger Williams, the land and meadows upon the two fresh rivers called, Mooshausick and Wonasquatucket, do now by these presents, establish and confirm the bounds of those lands from the river and fields at Pawtucket, the great hill of Neotaconkonitt on the north west, and the town of Masapauge on the west.   As also in consideration of the many kindnesses and services he hath continually done for us, both with our friends of Massachusetts, as also at Quin-ickicutt and Apaum or Plymouth, we do freely give unto him all that land from those rivers, reaching to Pawtuxet river, as also the grass and meadows upon the said Pawtuxet river.   In witness whereof we have hereunto set our hands.

The mark of Cannaunicus.

The mark of Meauntonomi.

In presence of

The mark of Seatash.

The mark of Assotemewit.

1639 Memorandum 3 mo. 9th day.   This was all again confirmed by Miantonomi, he acknowledged this his act and hand, up the streams of Pawtucket and Pawtuxet without limits, we might have for the use of our cattle.   Witness hereof

ROGER WILLIAMS.
BENEDICT ARNOLD."

There is a copy of a deed from Roger Williams, or rather an informal grant from him, known as his " Initial deed," in

which he grants his "loving friends and neighbors" equal
right and power of enjoyment and disposal of his purchase,
together with such as the major part shall admit into the
same fellowship of vote with us. This conveyance makes
no mention of the lands on the Pawtucket river. This
" Initial deed " was confirmed in technical language by deed
of 1661, which deed Mary, the wife of Roger Williams also
signed. The "Initial deed" was also again confirmed, the
names being written out in full, the 22, 10 mo. 1666, so
called.

During the first years of the colony the government was
as has been said, a pure democracy. Town meetings were
held monthly ; notice was required before any person could
be voted in as a member of the community ; a fine was imposed upon every person absent from any town meeting ;
the town granted the allotments of land to new-comers ;
every person was held to improve his or her grounds ;
every person was prohibited from selling " his field or lot
granted in our liberties to any person but an inhabitant,
without consent of the town." And the town assumed and
exercised the right of withholding the liberty of voting
from any one who should be guilty of "breach of cove-
nant " with the town.

The first departure from the principles and practice of a
pure democracy was made in 1640. It was now four years
since the six had landed at "What Cheer" rock; already
there were "many differences" in the small community
which had gathered about the first settlers ; but no differences which they were not willing equitably, peaceably and
economically to adjust. It may well have been also, that
although the number of the inhabitants was so small, they
found it necessary to contrive a more speedy method of
doing business than by general vote; and this all the more
that the town was as yet the legislature and the court. The
few bore the burdens; the many were indifferent; except

upon special occasions there was a lack of energy in the
government; special ability and determination were needed,
not only for special occasions but for the better ordering and
carrying out of the general and growing affairs of the town.
How cautiously and considerately the change was made is
apparent from the terms of the compact. Satisfied that
some portion of the sovereign power must be delegated,
the inhabitants parted with it charily, and hedged about the
authority of their representatives, forms, and the frequent
recurrence of elections in a way to prevent its abuse as
much as possible. It was an endeavor to infuse into the
government more certainty and security of operation, at the
same time retaining individual liberty, and the right of appeal to the whole body.

This characteristic and important document provides:
For the partition of the lands; and that the disposal of
the lands belonging to Providence as distinguished from
Pawtuxet shall be in the whole inhabitants by the choice of
five men for general disposal; that townsmen shall be received after six days' notice; that the five disposers have
the disposal also of the town's stock and all general things,
and that an appeal shall lie from the disposers to the general
town meeting. That as formerly hath been the liberties of
the town, so still to hold forth, liberty of conscience. That
differences and offences should be disposed of by arbitration.
But "all the whole inhabitants" should combine to assist
any man in the pursuit of any party delinquent. That
every man should have a deed of his lands. That the five
disposers meet monthly "upon general things," and be
chosen every quarter. That the general town meeting be
held every quarter. As moderate as was the delegation
of power to the disposers in point of time, it will be noticed
that the pure democracy resumed its authority every three
months; and that no man could be received without notice
to the inhabitants. And also that the liberty of conscience

was reiterated. The jealousy of delegated power could hardly further go, nor have we, nor has the world up to this day progressed beyond, nay! we have not come up to the judicious, judicial and inexpensive method of determining disputes initiated by our ancestors in 1640.

On the 14th day of March, 1644, Roger Williams obtained from the committee of the English Parliament, "The Incorporation of Providence Plantations in the Narragansett Bay in New England." By the charter full power was conferred upon the Plantations "to rule themselves and such others as shall hereafter inhabit within any part of the said tract of land, by such a form of civil government, as by voluntary consent of all or the greatest part of them shall be found most serviceable in their estates and condition; and to that end, to make and ordain such civil laws and constitutions, and to inflict such punishments upon transgressors, and for execution thereof so to place and displace officers of justice as they or the greatest part of them shall by free consent agree unto; Provided, nevertheless, that the said laws, constitutions and punishments for the civil government of the said plantations, be conformable to the laws of England, so far as the nature and constitution of the place will admit." Hitherto the three colonies of Providence, Acquedneck and Warwick had been entirely independent of each other. Isolated from the neighboring colonies in sentiment, and not united with each other in alliance against the Indians; without authoritative government as against the jurisdictional demands of the Massachusetts and Plymouth colonies, threatened on the one side by the Puritans, and on the other by the Indians, the charter of 1644 came to unite, to strengthen, to encourage and to dignify the Providence Plantations.

This charter emanated from an authority which none of the New England colonies could dispute; it was full and free; it ratified the "soul-liberty" of the people; it per-

2

mitted all reasonable and desirable freedom in legislation, in that the laws were not to be restricted to the rigid rules of the laws of England, but were to be made to conform to the "nature and constitution" of the country, the times, the circumstances and purposes of the incorporators and their fellows and successors. Roger Williams arrived in Boston with this charter on the 17th of September, 1644, and traversing the same parts through which he had first reached the shores of the Seekonk, he was met by the inhabitants of Providence in fourteen canoes, and escorted across the river amid the acclamations and rejoicings of a community which recognized in him its founder, administrator and most potent preserver and benefactor. A few years before Roger Williams had crossed that water with the five whom he had brought out of pity for their destitute condition. Then he was an exile; now he brought the charter of a State. Then he was welcomed only by the aborigines; now he was received by friends who appreciated his capacity and his goodness. Then he left civilization for the companionship of the Indians; now he returns to home, to a peaceable and orderly government, to the delights of civil and religious labor and advancement. Then he came as a solitary and dependent man; now he comes bearing the seal, and under the protection of the flag of England.

Notwithstanding the rejoicings at the reception in the fall of that year of the colony charter of 1644, for various reasons the government was not organized under it until May, 1647. On the 18th of that month not only the committees appointed by the towns of Providence, Portsmouth, Newport and Warwick, but a majority of the inhabitants of the said towns met at Portsmouth. It was in fact a meeting of the corporators to accept the charter, and to frame a government for the colony. They appointed a General Assembly of the whole colony to be holden annually, "if wind and weather hinder not," on the Tuesday after the 15th of May, at which the General Officers of the colony were to be chosen. These officers were a President, one Assistant for each town, a General Recorder, a Public Treasurer, and a General Sergeant; afterwards a General Attorney and a General Solicitor were added. Such of the colony as could not attend the General Assembly, had the right to send their votes for these officers by some other persons ; hence the origin of the terms prox, and proxy votes, as applied to mode of voting for State officers in Rhode Island, prior to the adoption of the Constitution. Each town had the nomination of one person for each of the offices of President, Recorder, Treasurer and Sergeant, and of two persons for each Assistant, from whom the election was to be made. The President and Assistants, composed the General Court of trials. They had jurisdiction over all aggravated offences, and in such matters as should be, by the town courts, referred to them as too weighty for themselves to determine, and also, of all disputes between different towns, or between citizens of different towns and strangers. They had two sessions each year. All questions of fact were determined by a jury of twelve men. The town courts had exclusive original jurisdiction over all causes between their own citizens. The President was Conservator of the Peace throughout the colony, and the Assistants in their respective towns. All legislative power was ultimately in the people, in General Assembly. Laws might be originated in the town, or in the General Assembly, but it was only by a vote of the majority of the electors of the colony that they were enacted into law to hold until the next General Assembly. It was declared in the code of laws which had been drawn up and sent to the several towns for examination, before the meeting of this General Assembly, and which was by it adopted, that: " The form of Government established in Providence Plantations is Democratic, that is to say, a government held by the free and voluntary consent of all or the greater part of the free inhabitants." The code contains nothing concerning religion. The first compact of the inhabitants of Providence concerning government was in, and as to "civil things only ; " the charter was silent as to religion, and this, the first code of laws enacted for the colony by its reticence permitted and guaranteed the largest liberty of conscience in religious matters. It was, indeed, expressive silence.

In 1650 it was "ordered that the Representatives Court, shall always consist of six discreet, able men, chosen out of each town, for the transacting of the affairs of the commonwealth." They were empowered to pass laws, which were to be sent to each town within six days, there to be considered and canvassed within three days. Those persons who disapproved of the proposed laws were to send their votes to the General Recorder within ten days, and unless it appeared that a majority of the freemen of the colony disapproved them, they remained in force as enacted by the Representatives. This was a marked improvement upon the laws of 1647 in that it stimulated the General Assembly to initiate laws for the general good, required only dissentients, in the towns, to vote and rendered more permanent the legislation of the colony.

At a special General Assembly holden in Warwick, in March, 1649, a charter was granted to the town of Providence. This charter gave the town the same freedom and powers within its own jurisdiction as the colonial charter had bestowed upon the colony.

In the summer of 1651, William Coddington returned from England, bringing with him a commission from the Council of State, signed by John Bradshaw, constituting him Governor of the Islands of Rhode Island and Canonicutt during his life. The colonial government under the charter was thus annihilated. The alarm in Providence and Warwick was almost equalled by the consternation on the islands. The only power left the people of Portsmouth and Newport was that they might appoint a council of six men to be approved by Coddington. In one word Coddington was appointed Dictator for life. John Clark was sent by the island towns, and Roger Williams by the towns of Providence and Warwick, to England to procure the abrogation of the authority granted to Coddington, and to attend to the interests of the colony. In the meantime the Court of Commissioners, being the committees of Providence and Warwick, met at Providence and determined to continue under the charter, making laws and choosing officers as before. And this was the technical and sensible course, for although the colonial government as under the charter was destroyed, the power given to Coddington by the Council of State did not repeal the charter so far as it related to, and affected Providence and Warwick.

And yet when in 1652, William Dyre arrived from England with the repeal of Coddington's authority, and wrote to the towns of Providence and Warwick, naming a day when he would meet all the freemen who chose to appear at Portsmouth, the committees of the towns of Providence and Warwick, although they carried a letter from the Commissioners of the towns to Portsmouth, would not agree that the General Assembly to hear the orders of Council should meet at Portsmouth. They insisted that the mainland towns were the Providence Plantations; that their charter had never been vacated. The island towns declared that as they formed the larger part of the colony, and had the greater interest in the matter, the Assembly should meet there. Both parties were right, and both were wrong. The mainland towns were the survivors under the charter; if it was to be revived in full they were certainly entitled to take precedence in the proceedings. On the other hand the allegation of the greater importance of Newport and Portsmouth was true. Both parties were wrong in permitting a mere matter of etiquette to prevent for a moment the reunion of the colony, and in postponing for an indefinite time the progress which could only be made by a common effort, and mutual good offices. It was only in May, 1654, that the General Assembly resumed its full and former functions. Only one General Assembly was held in that year, and in appearance and in form the colony was again one and united.

In September, 1658, Richard Cromwell succeeded to the supreme authority in England, as Lord Protector, upon the death of his father, Oliver Cromwell; and in May, 1659, the General Assembly addressed a letter to: "The most Serene and Illustrious, His Highness, the most renowned Richard, Lord Protector of the Commonwealth of England, Scotland and Ireland, and the dominions thereto belonging," asking a confirmation of their charter. It was never presented, as the Protector had resigned his power before it reached England. On the 8th day of June, 1660, Charles the Second entered London. The restoration was complete in form and in substance. The entry of the King into his kingdom was a triumphant one, all classes joining in receiving him as the guarantor of peace and order. Upon the receipt of this news a special session of the General Assembly was called to meet at Warwick. His Majesty's letter to Parliament, his declaration and proclamation were read and entered upon the records. The King was formally proclaimed the next morning in the presence of the General Assembly; it was ordered that all legal process should issue in his name, and a commission was sent to John Clarke, in London, confirming his position as agent for the colony, and desiring him to obtain a confirmation of the charter from the Crown.

From this time until 1663, the colony was, legally speaking, a law unto itself. The restoration of Charles technically abrogated the authority of the Parliamentary charter. Amid disputes, and dangers; the confusion of land titles, and the aggressions of the neighboring colonies, the inhabitants of the Providence Plantations waited in doubt for a conclusive letter from their agent. For twenty years the inhabitants had recognized as their sovereign authority a power which by the restoration of Charles was declared to be a rebellious, illegal and void power. The Parliament and Cromwell had not been treated as a government *de facto* in the sense in which one government accepts the actual government of another nation; they had been appealed to, and their action asked as though they were *de jure* the sovereign power. The Plantations were in bad odor with their neighbors, and their neighbors were strong. Both Massachusetts and Connecticut claimed jurisdiction in Rhode Island territory, and Massachusetts was well known and had great influence in England. The liberty of Rhode Island, the Puritans deemed licentiousness. The principles upon which her government was founded were in utter opposition to the monarchical theories of England as well as to the doctrine of the divine right of Kings, of Charles Stuart. Her very freedom in religious matters made her the opprobrium of the other colonies, as it would have astonished and dismayed the church and sectarists of England. And Mr. Clarke, in his addresses to King Charles asserted that the people of Rhode Island "have it much in their hearts, if they may be permitted to hold forth a lively experiment, that a flourishing civil state may stand, yea, and be best maintained, and that among English spirits, with full liberty in religious concernments." A potent argument one would think to address to the Merry Monarch!

The long continued efforts of Clarke were at last successful. In November, 1663, the General Court of Commissioners—the General Assembly, met at Newport, for the last time under the Parliamentary patent to receive the Royal Charter of Charles II. Then ended the government of the colony under the charter of the Council of State. There was no longer the incorporation of Providence Plantations. The charter of 1644, had nevertheless been of inestimable service. It had bestowed upon an aggregation of individuals a political existence; it had thrown over and around them in their direst need the protection of a powerful nation; it had consolidated the Rhode Island colonies in a degree which enabled them to make progress in order and in security. It did not meet all the necessities of the case, any more than did the Confederation of the States fulfill the functions of the national Constitution, but it was a step in the right direction, and an immense gain over the hitherto almost anarchic condition of the towns as to their relations with each other. Less than thirty years have elapsed since Roger Williams first set foot upon Rhode Island soil; a large territory, including one of the fairest islands of the sea has been acquired; government has been established; the six have grown into a goodly number; there are villages, and plenty, and liberty, and an independence of spirit which has descended in direct line, and ample vigor to our own times. Already self-government was the proved rule as well as theory; already every principle of liberty regulated by law had been enunciated; already the towns were the schools of statesmanship, and already the Rhode Island character had assumed the traits of energy, activity, openness of speech and a self esteem which at once and equally ignored interference on the part of others, and bowed to the dictates of conscience.

This charter of King Charles was all that could have been desired. Under it the State was an absolute sovereignty. No oath of allegiance was required. Religious freedom was guaranteed. The title of the Indians to the soil was recognized, as Roger Williams and his fellow townsmen had always recognized it. It declares " that noe person within sayd colonye, at any tyme hereafter, shall bee any wise molested, punished, disquited, or called in question, for any difference in opinioue in matters of religion which doe not actually disturb the civill peace of our sayd colonye." This charter of, and from a monarch who believed in his divine right to govern, was expressly republican in its character. Under this charter the people of Rhode Island lived and prospered for one hundred and eighty years. When it was abrogated in 1843, it was the oldest constitutional charter in the world. It survived the Stuart dynasty. It remained intact through the Revolutionary war. It sufficed when, and after the State entered the Union. During its existence the commonwealth grew in population, in wealth, in influence in a degree which equalled the firmness with which it maintained its original and distinctive principles. Now for the first time the Assistants were invested with legislative power by the charter, and acted conjointly with the deputies. Upon a question arising whether under the terms of the charter the State Magistrates, or Council, should be elected by the freemen in town meeting, or by the General Assembly, it was decided that the right of electing these officers should vest in the freemen. Here we see the old and ineradicable opposition to the delegation of power, unless in case of overpowering necessity.

The name of "Rhode Island and Providence Plantations," with the word "Hope" above the anchor, was adopted, or rather continued, upon the seal of the colony. In 1664 it was provided that a plurality vote should elect the general officers. The General Assembly exercised judicial as well as legislative powers, and as under the first patent the President and assistants were executive officers. By the royal charter the governor and council became *ex officio* legislators in common with the deputies, and all alike exercised judicial powers. They met together as one House of Assembly. It is proper to notice also, that as late as 1672, there was a prevalent feeling that the acts of a given Assembly were not

3

binding beyond the next session. And at the May session of this year a striking example of popular mutability of sentiment was afforded by the repeal of every act passed at the preceding April session. For an account of the Indian war initiated by the neighboring colonies, and from which Rhode Island suffered so much the reader is referred to the history of the State. Suffice it to say that the Indians burned the town of Providence, and spared Roger Williams. In 1682, it was decided by the General Assembly that the town councils might reject any person as an inhabitant of the town, who should fail to give bonds satisfactory to a majority of the council; and if any one being warned by the council to leave the town, should fail to do so, a warrant for his removal might be issued to the constable, and in case of his return to the town he should be subject to fine or whipping.

The claims of the Connecticut and Plymouth colonies to the soil and jurisdiction of portions of Rhode Island at length culminated in the appointment of a commission by King Charles, for examining and enquiring into the claims and titles to the King's Province, or Narragansett Country. The summons of the commission included in the subject of their inquiry the territory between the rivers of Providence and Pauquatuck, the islands of Prudence, Cannonicut, Patience, or any other island which were or were reputed to have belonged to the Narragansett Country. There seems to have been little question made save as to the Province; and the jurisdiction of this was bestowed upon Connecticut, and the "propriety of the soil" to the Atherton Company. The death of Charles II., and the proclamation of his brother James II. were inauspicious events for Rhode Island. Other claimants to the Narragansett Country laid their claims before the Crown, and they were referred to the Board of Trade. The settlers were uneasy and belligerent. A crisis was at hand. A *quo warranto* was issued against Rhode Island as against other colonies, for the purpose of revoking its charter. Two days later a President and Council were appointed to govern Massachusetts, New Hampshire, Maine and King's Province. Upon the arrival of the *quo warranto*, the General Assembly being met, and a large number of persons present it was determined not to stand suit with the King, but to proceed by humble address to his Majesty, asking a continuance of their charter privileges.

Dudley, the new Governor, or President of the Council created a provisional government, to continue only till the plan of consolidating all New England under one royal governor could be perfected. This was done by the appointment of Sir Edmund Andros, formerly governor of New York, to the supreme authority by royal commission. Andros was authorized to demand the surrender of the charter, and to take the colony of Rhode Island and Providence Plantations under his government. And the power given him was almost absolute. By letter from Boston, dated December, 1686, he appointed Walter Clark, Jo. Sanford, John Coggeshall, Walter Newbury, John Greene, Richard Arnold, and John Albrough, to be members of his Council. The colonial government was subverted. A second time had the charter of her liberties been taken from Rhode Island. She was now reduced to a mere province in the broad dominion of the Captain General, and Governor in Chief of New England. She returned to her system of town government. The last act of the General Assembly had been to provide that it "should be lawful for the freemen of each town in this colony to meet together and appoint five, or more or fewer, days in the year for their assembling together, as the freemen of each town shall conclude to be convenient, for the managing the affairs of their respective towns." Inasmuch as Andros and his Council had full legislative, judicial and executive authority, the legal value of this last act of the General Assembly is much more questionable than is the patriotic spirit which prompted it.

Upon receiving the news of the accession of William and Mary to the throne of England, in 1689, a letter cautiously worded was sent from Newport among the people recommending them to assemble there, "before the day of annual election by charter," to consult what course should be adopted. The freemen of the colony assembled and put forth a declaration of their reasons for resuming the charter government. But, although the government was reorganized it remained for ten months without an acknowledged governor. Walter Clarke was too cautious to accept the office in the uncertain condition of public affairs. This act of resumption was afterward sanctioned by the crown.

At the May session, 1696, the House of deputies was constituted a distinct body; a lower house of assembly, with power to choose its own Speaker, and Clerk. It thus became a coördinate branch of the legislature with the assistants, each house having a veto upon the proceedings of the other; and thus has it ever since remained. And not even a limited veto power has ever been conferred upon the Governor. The first instance of the deputies resolving themselves into a committee of the whole for the preparation of business occurred at this session. Nor was the government again established in its chartered authority. The charter was not again to be suspended or questioned, until under circumstances then unforeseen, and doubtless unimaginable it should be superseded by the will of the people in the attempt to secure a still broader republicanism.

A census was taken in 1730. The population of the colony was then, Whites, 15,302; Negroes, 1,648; Indians, 985; total, 17,935. Of Providence, Whites, 3,707; Negroes, 128; Indians, 81; total, 3,916. Of Newport, Whites, 3,843; Negroes, 649; Indians, 248; total, 4,640. This census probably included the inhabitants of "the Gore," now Cumberland. Roger Williams died sometime between January 18, and May 10, 1683. For nearly half a century he had been the foremost man in a community which from weakness had grown to strength; which had seen the seed of liberty it planted in doubt and fear, grow to a tree of such goodly proportions that its shelter attracted the good and wise from abroad. Amid difficulties which would have appalled the stoutest hearts, and discouraged any but the most courageous and faithful minds, Roger Williams clung with the same determination to his doctrine of democratic government, and to his theory of the right of perfect liberty in religious concerns. Never seeking repose from labor, his enemies within and without Rhode Island permitted him no rest either of body or of mind. He was generous, as his disposition of his lands shows; he was firm, as is evinced by the tenor of his whole life; he was honest, as the natives always testified, and as none could gainsay. He was a scholar, a statesman, a patriot and a Christian. He impressed upon Rhode Island characteristics, social, political and religious, which to-day are her support and pride.

CHAPTER II.

A T the session of the General Assembly, held at Newport by adjournment, in February, 1730, (O. S.) the town of Smithfield was incorporated. The preamble to the act is in the words following: "Forasmuch as the Out Lands of the Town of Providence are large, and replenished with Inhabitants sufficient to make and erect three Townships besides the Town of Providence and the Land lies convenient for the same; which will be of great Ease and Benefit to the Inhabitants of said Land, in transacting and negotiating the prudential Affairs of their Town, which for some Time past has been very heavy and burthensome;" and Smithfield, Scituate and Glocester were separated into independent townships. It was provided that the towns were to "have each their proportion of the interest of the Bank money appropriated to the use of the towns of this colony, according to the sums that the lands lying in each town are mortgaged for; and that money the town treasurer of Providence has advanced for the town before the division thereof, be repaid him out of the whole interest money, before division thereof be made."

The significance of this latter clause we shall discover as we proceed.

The territory thus set off comprised seventy-three square miles of land. It was bounded on the East by the Blackstone river; on the South by Johnston and North Providence; on the West by Glocester, and on the North by the

State of Massachusetts. At the time of the division of the town the western boundary was the East line of Glocester and Burrillville, the latter town having been set off from Glocester. Bounded on one side by the most important river in the State, save Providence river, it included within its limits the Branch, the Moshassuck, the Woonasquatucket and the Crook Fall rivers, besides other smaller streams which benefited and beautified it. It presented in its natural physical features a diversified and attractive aspect. Near its northern extremity rose Woonsocket Hill, the highest land in the State, towering nearly six hundred feet above the level of the sea. Its hills were clothed with a luxuriant growth of Oak, Walnut, Ash, Chestnut and Birch trees; its valleys were many of them rich in soil; the plains were easily cultivated; to the hardy pioneer, who sought to derive from nature a homely but comfortable and independent subsistence, Smithfield offered charming scenery, good land, pure water, an abundance of timber and ready access to the town, and to navigable waters. In its lime stone quarries it possessed a source of usefulness and emolument which was early utilized, and still remains in its development and permanence a most important industry. Originally a purely agricultural district, we shall find that in its then almost unrecognized, but eventually valuable water power, it owned a source of wealth which was to change the character of its pursuits, to swell, and affect the habits of its population and to cause an accession of prop erty of which the early settlers had, and could have no pos sible conception. At the time of its incorporation Smithfield was very sparsely settled, its inhabitants being mainly families who had pushed out into the country from Providence, and who were wholly in accord in their social, political and religious ideas, with the early settlers of that town. Smithfield, was, indeed, only a prolongation of Providence. The men who organized the town were men who had been famil-

iar, and who were moved with the sentiments of Roger Wil-
iams, and the freemen of Providence. They were actuated
by the same spirit of independence, the same love of, and for
self-government, the same doctrine of the liberty of conscience. They were sufficiently learned to act intelligently,
and they were sufficiently strong to carry on, and out their
theories. They leaned upon nobody; they were industrious, economical, conservative and thoughtful. Their territory was large; their principles fixed; in separating from the
parent town they undertook that closer management of their
affairs for which they were eminently capable. They were
among the first to take their portion, and they made such
good use of it that for an hundred and forty years Smithfield was a progressive, influential, important and deservedly-
esteemed town.

The record of the first town meeting is as follows, the
orthography being conformed to the usage of the present
day: "At a town meeting called by warrant under the
hands and seals of Joseph Arnold and Jonathan Sprague,
Jr., Esqs., Justices of the Peace, and held at the house of
Captain Valentine Whitman in Smithfield, in the County of
Providence, &c., on the 17, day of March, Anno Domini,
1730 or 31; whereof Mr. Jonathan Sprague, Jr., was chosen
moderator of said meeting, and Richard Sayles was chosen
town clerk, at said meeting, and John Arnold chosen the
first town councilman at said meeting, and Captain Joseph
Mowry chosen the second town councilman, Thomas Steere
chosen the third town councilman, Samuel Aldrich chosen
the fourth town councilman, John Mowry chosen the fifth
town councilman, Benjamin Smith chosen the sixth town
councilman; John Sayles chosen at said meeting town treasurer; Uriah Mowry chosen town sergeant at aforesaid meeting. Joseph Arnold, Jun., chosen sealer and packer at said
meeting; David Comstock chosen the first constable, Elisha
Steere chosen the second constable, and Joseph Herendeen,

Jr., chosen the third constable. Captain Valentine Whitman and Thomas Smith and Joshua Winsor and Jeremiah Arnold were chosen overseers of the poor of the town. Job Arnold and John Smith, son of Joseph Smith 'Juyner' chosen surveyors of the highways. Hezekiah Comstock and Daniel Arnold and John Dexter Jun. and Jonathan Sprague minor, chosen fence viewers. Joseph Bagley and Daniel Matthewson chosen hemp viewers. John Whitman chosen pound keeper. John Wilkinson and Charles Sherlock chosen hog constables. Richard Sayles accepted and was engaged according to law to the office of town clerk for the ensuing year before Jonathan Sprague, Justice, the day and year above said. The town councilmen that were chosen did all accept and was engaged according to law to the office of town councilman, before Jonathan Sprague, Justice, the day and year above said. John Sayles did accept and was engaged according to law to the office of town treasurer, before Jonathan Sprague, Justice. Uriah Mowry did accept and was engaged according to law to the office of town sergeant. David Comstock and Elisha Steere and Joseph Herendeen Jr., did all accept and were engaged according to law to the offices of constables. Hezekiah Comstock and Daniel Arnold and John Dexter Jr., and Jonathan Sprague minor, did all accept and were engaged according to law to the office of fence viewers. Captain Valentine Whitman and Thomas Smith and Jeremiah Arnold all accepted and were engaged according to law to office of overseers of the poor. Job Arnold and John Smith both accepted and engaged according to law to the office of highway surveyors. Joseph Arnold Jr., accepted and was engaged according to law to the office of sealer and packer. John Whitman accepted and engaged according to law to the office of pound keeper. Daniel Matthewson and Joseph Bagley both accepted and were engaged according to law to the office of hemp viewers. It was voted at said meeting that the 27,

4

day of April next is the day perfixed for the freemen of the town of Smithfield to meet together at the house of John Sayles in Smithfield in order to choose Representatives to send to Newport, next May Session, and also to send in their proxies for the General Officers of this colony, and also to do other business as is necessary for said town."

On the 23, of March, 1731, (N. S.) the town meeting chose its deputies to the General Assembly; provided its quota of jurors, for a settlement with the town of Providence, and voted a bounty for killing wild-cats and wolves. In 1738, a pair of stocks was built, and a whipping post erected near the house of John Sayles.

In 1738, the town took a most important step in developing its resources, and providing for the comfort and convenience of its inhabitants. This was the passage of an highway act. Before this time there had been, in Rhode Island, no other law upon this subject than the laws of England, which were of course but ill adapted to the circumstances in which the then inhabitants of Smithfield found themselves. The "act" passed by the town was drawn with great care, and a precision which is evidence of the capacity of those who adopted it for self-government. It provided for the appointment of surveyors, and made it their duty to inspect the roads within the limits of their jurisdiction, and enough of them were appointed to care for the highways throughout the town; specific provision was made for the amount and character of the work to be done, and every male person an inhabitant of the town, twenty-one years of age, and able-bodied, except apprentices, slaves and idiots, was to work on the highways six days in the year, and eight hours a day.

In 1748, the population of Smithfield was four hundred and fifty persons; the town was divided into sixteen highway districts, to be worked by the persons hereinafter enumerated, the person first named in each district being surveyor.

District No 1, began at Patience Arnold's, so to extend northwesterly over the Branch River, and all the roads west and northwest of said river. The citizens therein were:

Daniel Comstock, jr.,	Samuel Buxton,	Azariah Comstock,
Hezadiah Comstock,	Benjamin Buxton,	Jonathan Reed,
Ichabod Comstock,	Joseph Buxton,	Thomas Cruff,
Anthony Comstock,	Joseph Buffum,	Thomas Cruff, jr.,
Richard Sprague,	Joseph Kelley,	Samuel Cruff,
Amos Sprague,	Providence Williams,	Jacob Read,
Benjamin Buffum,	John Sprague,	Benj. Buffum, jr.,
Samuel Goldthwaite,	Daniel Comstock,	Daniel Sprague,
Israel Phillips,	Benjamin Boyce,	Nathaniel Staples,
Benjamin Thompson,	Adam Harkness,	Samuel Buxton, jr.

District No. 2, began at Samuel Aldrich (near Union village), so down to where the new road turns out of the old, and by the new and the old road to where they intersect on the Hill, a little southeast from the Little River Bridge—also, the cross road by Benjamin Paine and Uriah Mowry (on Sayles's Hill):

John Sayles,	Daniel Sayles,	Henry Mowry,
Uriah Mowry,	Joshua Phillips,	Edward Mitchell,
Benjamin Paine,	David Herrendeen,	Elisha Mowry,
Capt. Richard Sayles,	Jonathan Phillips,	Daniel Walling.
Richard Sayles, jr,,	Stephen Sly,	
Elisha Sayles,	Ebenezer Thornton,	

District No. 3, began at Locusquesset Brook (near Lime Rock), and so up the Highway, till it comes to where two roads meet on the Hill, a little southeast from the Little River Bridge:

Peter Bellowe, jr.,	Jabez Brown,	John Bellowe, jr.,
John Whitman,	Noah Whitman,	Jonathan Bellowe,
Preserved Harris,	Nicholas Brown,	Benjamin Brown,
Jonathan Harris,	John Bellowe,	Manasses Kimton,
Valentine Whitman,	Samuel Bellow,	Christopher Bullock.

District No. 4, began at Locusquesset Brook to Providence line, also the Cross Road by Jonathan Arnold's, beginning at the old highway by the Lime Kiln, to end where said highway intersects with the highway that goes by Dr. Jenckes—also the Cross Road from Abraham Scott to Pawtucket River:

Wm. Whipple, jr.,   Benjamin Smith,   Jeremiah Arnold, jr.,
Jeremiah Mowry,   Jonathan Arnold,   William Brown,
Nathaniel Bucklin,   Job Arnold,   John Arnold,
Benjamin Medbury,   Amos Arnold,   Nathan Tucker,
Wm. Jenckes, Esq.,   William Bensley,   Abraham Scott,
Benjamin Arnold,   John Whipple,   John Weatherhead,
Samuel Bagley,   Manassah Kelley,   Andrew Young,
Anthony Whipple,   Benjamin Medbury,   Christopher Jenckes.
Jerrh. Weatherhead,   Caleb Arnold,
William Whipple,   Jeremiah Arnold,

District No. 5, began at the Old Quaker Meeting House, so northeasterly and northerly to Thomas Lapham's (near Albion):

John Dexter,   John Wilkinson, jr.,   Ephraim Whipple,
Jonathan Sprague,   Thos. Lapham, Esq.,   Samuel Smith.
William Sprague,   Capt. Job Whipple,
John Wilkinson,   Stephen Whipple,

District No. 6, began at Thomas Lapham's, and so north, to Woonsocket Falls. (The River Road from Albion up):

Joseph Lapham,   Caleb Shrefe,   Israel Wilkinson,
Azariah Phillips,   James Jillson,   John Rogers,
William Gully,   David Patt,   Capt. Wm. Sprague.
Elisha Dillingham,   Aaron Day,

District No. 7, began at Daniel Wilbur's to Providence line—also,
from same place to Christopher Brown's:

Benjamin Cook,   Obadiah Olney,   Daniel Wilbur,
Thomas Woodward,   Job Chase,   Capt. Richard Harris,
Robert Young,   Baulston Brayton,   Jeremiah Harris,
Samuel Tucker,   William Olney,   Christopher Brown,
Maturin Ballowe,   John Jenckes,   Abiah Angell,
Peter Ballowe,   William Bradbury,   John Olney.
Maturin Ballowe, jr.,   Daniel Bradbury,
James Mussey,   William Pullen,

District No. 8, began at saw mill by James Appleby, to Thomas
Sayles, and from Elisha Cook's, towards Providence line, till it comes
to Ebenezer Herrendeen's:

Elisha Cook,	William Baets,	Joseph Mowry, 3d,
Joseph Page,	Henry Blackmar,	Silvanus Sayles,
Ebenezer Herrendeen,	John Blackmar,	Capt. Daniel Mowry.
Thomas Sayles,	Theophilus Blackmar,	
Stephen Sayles,	Aaron Herrendeen,	

District No. 9, began at Glocester line, west of John Sayles, jr., so easterly by Othonial Matthewson, thence northeast to Woonsocket Falls — also a piece from Thomas Sayles to aforesaid road:

Othonial Matthewson,	Mikel Phillips,	Samuel Aldrich,
Daniel Smith,	James Walling,	Samuel Tucker,
John Comstock,	Ananias Mowry,	Thomas Smith,
Jeremiah Brown,	John Sayles, jr.,	Cornelius Walling.
Daniel Phillips,	John Smith,	Reuben Aldrich.

District No. 10, began at Ebenezer Herrendeen, down to Daniel Wilbur:

Thomas Herrendeen,	Thomas Shippe,	Joseph Herrendeen,
Henry Morton,	Obadiah Herrendeen,	Jos. Herrendeen, jr.,
Jacob Smith,	Nathan Shippe,	Francis Herrendeen,
Thomas Shippe, jr.,	Benjamin Ballard,	Gideon Pain,
Christopher Shippe,	John Young,	Jeremiah Ballard.
William Havens,	Silas Tucker,	

District No. 11, began at Providence line, near Isaac White's, to the "Logway," also the Cross Road from Daniel Angell, to the Island Road:

Thomas Steere,	Philip Smith,	Ezekiel Angell,
Joseph Chillson,	Daniel Angell,	James Young,
Noah Smith's widow,	John Angell,	Amos Keach,
Daniel Smith,	Thomas Broadway,	Thomas Owen,
Jonathan Smith,	Hezekiah Sprague,	Major William Smith.
John Phillips,	John Smith, jr.,	Daniel Smith.
Elisha Smith,	Job Angell,	

District No. 12, began at Abraham Smith's barn, so southeast by Smith's house, to Providence line:

Leland Smith,	Enoch Barnes,	Jos. Smith, son of Jos.,
Peter Barnes,	John Barnes,	John Treadwen,
Nathan Barnes,	Joseph Smith,	Joseph Page.

District No. 13, began at the corner of Abraham Smith's fence, near the Baptist Meeting House, thence, northerly by Abraham Smith's, so up the "Logway" to Glocester line, also the cross road, beginning at the saw mill by his house, thence southerly to aforesaid road:

James Appleby,	Thomas Beadle,	John Aldrich,
Capt. Joseph Mowry,	David Arnold,	Stephen Goodspeed,
George Place,	Silvanus Aldrich,	Oliver Mowry,
Joseph Mowry, jr.,	Peter Aldrich,	Abraham Smith.

District No. 14, began at Glocester line, by Widow Steere's, to Providence line, all below Joseph Carpenter's:

Samuel Aldrich, jr.,	David Evans, jr.,	Joseph Smith, jr.,
Robert Latham,	Joseph Aldrich,	Thomas Inches,
Joseph Carpenter,	Job Potter,	Joshua Winsor,
Zachariah Rhodes,	Samuel Winsor,	John Winsor.
David Evans,	Hezekiah Steere,	

District No. 15, began at Glocester line, a little west of Benjamin Wilkinson, thence down to Providence line — also from Resolved Waterman's, thence southwesterly to Glocester line, by Snake Hill:

Abraham Winsor,	Samuel Irons,	Abel Potter,
Benjamin Wilkinson,	Robert Staples,	Resolved Waterman.
Benjamin Wright,	Andrew Waterman,	
Joshua Winsor, jr.,	Daniel Eddy,	

District No. 16, began at Glocester, line near Daniel Matthewson, thence northeasterly by his house to Wainsocket Falls, till it meets Cumberland in the middle of the Bridge. Also, beginning at Patience Arnold's, thence down to District No. 2. (This was a portion of the Great Road to Sayles Hill, and South Main Street, west to Burrillville):

Nathan Staples,	Joseph Comstock,	Seth Arnold,
Seth Cook,	Hezadiah Comstock,	Moses Arnold,
Nathaniel Eddy,	David Comstock, Esq.,	Abraham Loja,
Elisha Arnold,	Thomas Man,	Philip Loja,
Richard Arnold,	Capt. Daniel Arnold,	Jeremiah Comstock,
Stephen Arnold,	Widow Patience "	Oliver Man,
Samuel Cook,	Lieut. Thos. Arnold,	Caleb Aldrich.
John Man, jr.,	William Arnold, Esq.,	
Samuel Aldrich, 3d,	John Arnold,	

The business transacted by the first Town Council, at its first meeting was eminently significant. A committee was appointed to arrange the monetary matters between the town and the town of Providence; sundry persons were ordered to be cited before the council " to give their reasons why they inhabit in the town of Smithfield without admittance of said town council;" some persons were ordered removed from the town. Whether the strict supervision exercised over new comers was stimulated by a fear of having them to support, or because of a regard for the morals of the town, certain it is that the diligence used to ascertain the fitness of the aspirant for a permanent residence was both active and effectual. In this regard there was in Smithfield, in those days, nothing known of the law's delay. The person cited, if recalcitrant was forthwith put out of the town by the Sergeant; if he returned he was ordered to pay a fine within one hour, or be stripped naked " from the waist upward " and whipped. It is a very gratifying fact that the record shows that when one Phebe Thornton a transient person, was ordered by the council to pay a fine evidently far beyond her means, on the instant, or be stripped and whipped, that good Quaker, Thomas Steere, so many years President of the council, was not present. The town stocks and the whipping post were located in his section of the town, but careful as the Friends were of their own and the town's money, there is the religious and record reason for believing that the wandering Phebe was not scourged in accordance with the vote or sentiment of the well-to do, and public spirited Thomas.

At a special town meeting, held on the sixteenth of September, 1774, Capt. Arnold Paine, and William Winsor, Esqs., were chosen a committee to repair to the town of Boston, there to inspect into the circumstances of the poor of said town, and make report on the 10th day of October next. Capt. William Potter, Peleg Arnold and Stephen

Whipple were appointed a committee to receive the directions given by the inhabitants for the relief of the poor of Boston.

At a town meeting held on the 10th of October, 1774, the committee aforenamed made a verbal report and the town "welcome for the above service, for which the town returns them thanks." "Whereupon it is Voted, that subscription papers be drawn up for the purpose of gaining support for the poor sufferers of Boston, and delivered into the hands of the committee already appointed for that purpose, and that William Potter, Peleg Arnold and Stephen Whipple do the service appointed gratis; to which they in this meeting agreed in person; and that the subscription papers with receipts be returned to the town clerk's office of this town, to the intent that full and ample satisfaction may be made in that behalf."

The result of this action will be seen by a perusal of the following letter, directed to Daniel Mowry, Jr., Town Clerk:

BOSTON, Nov. 2d, 1774.

GENTLEMEN:

By the hands of Capt. Stephen Whipple and Mr. William Potter, the Committee of Donations received your very acceptable present of one hundred and fifty sheep. The Committee, in behalf of the Town, return our grateful acknowledgments to our kind and generous benefactors, the patriotic inhabitants of Smithfield and Johnston. Such bounties greatly refresh our spirits, and encourage us to persevere in the glorious cause of true, constitutional freedom and liberty. We consider the cause as common, and therefore a cause in the defence of which, all North America ought to be united ; and it affords us, as it must every true-hearted American, a peculiar pleasure, that such union prevails at this day, as bodes well to the rights and liberties of North America, civil and religious.

What judgment are we to form respecting those who would affect to be calm and unconcerned spectators, in this day of trouble and distress. But what shall we think and say of those who are constantly endeavoring, in a private, and when they dare, more open manner, to carry into execution a plan the most detestable, and calculated for the destruction of everything accounted valuable and dear in the eyes of Americans. Surely, then, Americans must, they will, exert themselves to their utmost at such a day as this.

The inhabitants of this town are called, in providence, to stand, as it were in the front of the battle. We have reason, in the first place, to be thankful to God, who hath thus far helped us, and nextly, to our generous and kind benefactors, by their affectionate letters, as well as their timely donations. May the Lord reward them. We greatly need wisdom, direction, prudence, zeal, patience and resolution. Our Christian friends may, by their prayers to God, contribute much towards a happy issue of these severe trials, and those mercies which are the fruit of the prayers of faith will prove mercies indeed. But we have not time to enlarge.

Inclosed is a printed half sheet respecting the conduct of the Committee on the improvement of the charities of our friends, which we hope will be to their satisfaction.

Gentlemen, your much obliged friends and fellow-countrymen.

DAVID JEFFRIES. } *Per order of the*
Committee of Donations.

1775. At a town meeting held on the 20th day of February, 1775, Stephen Arnold, Jr., Andrew Waterman, Thomas Aldrich, Elisha Mowry, Jr., and Uriah Alverson were appointed a committee of inspection, agreeable to the eleventh article of the Continental Congress, and Daniel Mowry, Jr., and Othniel Matthewson were appointed a committee to receive the town's quota of fire-arms, according to act of government, and deliver the same to the three present captains of the foot companies in this town according to the muster rolls in number. In June of the same year Stephen Whipple, Joseph Jencks, Daniel Angell, Arnold Paine, Peleg Arnold, Andrew Waterman, and Elisha Mowry, Jr., were chosen to collect one hundred fire-arms, to put them in proper repair for battle at the expense of the town, to be then lodged; one-third part at the dwelling house of Capt. Joseph Jencks; one-third part at Col. Elisha Mowry's, and the other third part at Peleg Arnold's; to be and remain for the use of the town on any invasion that may happen; and that

5

William Potter, Joseph Jencks, and Sylvanus Sayles be a committee to prize said guns. Immediately thereafter, at an adjourned meeting, it was voted that all the fire arms within the train-band of the first company in the town, be collected at the dwelling house of Capt. Joseph Jencks within the week; those of the second and third companies to be also collected, "in order to collect one hundred of the best quality to be equipped for use immediately."

The aforesaid arms not having been collected in accordance with the vote of the town, it was at an adjourned meeting, held on the first lawful day after the expiration of the time within which said arms should have been deposited as aforesaid, voted: "that the committees, or any of them are requested to take forthwith said number of guns from any of the inhabitants of the town."

In February, 1775, Stephen Arnold, Jr., Andrew Waterman, Thomas Aldrich, Elisha Mowry, Jr., and Uriah Alverson were chosen a committee of inspection, agreeable to the eleventh article of the Continental Congress. And Daniel Mowry, Jr., and Othniel Mathewson were appointed to receive the quota of fire-arms, and deliver the same to the captains of the three foot companies.

At a special town meeting, held in June, 1775, Stephen Whipple, Joseph Jenckes, Daniel Angell, Arnold Paine, Peleg Arnold, Jacob Comstock, Abraham Winsor, Andrew Waterman and Elisha Mowry, Jr., were chosen a committee to collect one hundred fire-arms, and the same to put in proper repair for battle. One-third of these arms were to be lodged at the house of Capt. Joseph Jenckes, one-third at the house of Col. Elisha Mowry, and one-third at the house of Mr. Peleg Arnold.

In December, the town council was directed to convene, and make a list of all the inhabitants obliged by law to equip themselves, and unable to purchase fire-arms and appurtenances. In February, 1776, nineteen new fire-arms were ordered to be purchased. In June, Elisha Mowry, Jr., was appointed to receive the salt appropriated by government for the use of the town. In September, Capt. Samuel Day, Capt. David Eddy, and Capt. James Smith were severally directed to raise each, their due proportion of thirty-nine men to march to Newport; and forty-eight shillings bounty was offered to recruits with guns, and well accoutred; and thirty-six shillings to each recruit not equipped. At the August town meeting it was voted:

"Whereas there is now a bill received by the General Assembly of this Colony in order to be passed into a law relative to the importation of negro and mulatto slaves, as also several other matters relating to negro and mulatto slaves; a copy thereof being present: therefore it is voted by this town meeting that the Representatives for this town use their uttermost endeavors to pass said bill in to a law of this Colony."

At the May session of the General Assembly, 1776, certain towns were supplied with powder and lead; and to Smithfield was apportioned 200 pounds of powder and 400 pounds of lead.

At the June session a census of the population was ordered, and Daniel Mowry, Jr., was the committee for this town. All the salt in the Colony was directed to be divided among the several towns at the rate of six shillings per bushel, "for cash only," and Smithfield was allowed 150 bushels. A new distribution of salt was ordered, Smithfield being allowed 400½ bushels.

This year a hospital was provided "to introduce the small pox by inoculation."

1776. In May, 1776, John Sayles, Esq., was Assistant, and Daniel Mowry, Jr., Esq., and Capt. Andrew Waterman were Deputies. The General Assembly repealed the "Act of Allegiance," preceding the repeal by this Preamble: "Whereas in all States existing by Compact, Protection and Allegiance are reciprocal, the latter being due only in consequence of the former: And whereas GEORGE the Third, King of *Great Britain*, forgetting his Dignity, regardless of the Compact most solemnly entered into, ratified and confirmed, to the Inhabitants of this Colony, by His illustrious Ancestors, and till of late fully recognized by Him—and entirely departing from the Duties and Character of a good King, instead of protecting, is endeavoring to destroy the good People of this Colony, and of all the United Colonies, by sending Fleets and Armies to America, to Confiscate our Property, and spread Fire, Sword and Desolation, throughout our Country, in order to compel us to submit to the most debasing and detestable Tyranny; whereby we are obliged by Necessity, and it becomes our highest Duty, to use every Means, with which God and Nature have furnished us, in support of our invaluable Rights and Privileges; to oppose that Power which is exerted only for our Destruction."

Be it therefore enacted by this General Assembly, and by the Authority thereof it is enacted, that an Act intituled 'An Act for the more effectual securing to His Majesty the Allegiance of his Subjects in this his Colony and Dominion of Rhode Island and Providence Plantations," be, and the same is hereby, repealed. The act then went on to provide for the necessary changes in the terms of the Commissions for offices, civil and military; and that in all suits and processes in law, reference to the King should be omitted, and they should run in the name, and by the authority of "The Governor and Company of the English Colony of Rhode Island and Providence Plantations.'"

Stephen Hopkins and William Ellery were appointed delegates to the Continental Congress.

With that same caution which distinguished the early Rhode Islanders in delegating, or parting with authority, the delegates were instructed by the General Assembly, as to the extent of their powers, and as to the sentiments of the legislature.

They were to consult with the delegates of, and from the other colonies, upon the most proper measures for promoting and confirming the strictest Union and Consideration between the said United Colonies, for exerting their whole strength and force to annoy the common enemy, and to secure to the said Colonies their rights and liberties, both civil and religious, * * * * taking the greatest care to secure to this Colony, in the strongest and most perfect manner, its present established form, and all the powers of government, so far as relates to its internal police and conduct of our own affairs, civil and religious.

A committee, one of whom was Andrew Waterman, was appointed to procure, and send immediately to Newport, as many iron, or shod shovels, as could be got, and to procure to be made as soon as possible, fifty good spades.

Elisha Mowry, Jr., Esq., was chosen Lieutenant Colonel of the Second Regiment of Militia, in the County of Providence.

The following were the officers of the three Smithfield Militia companies:

FIRST COMPANY.

Captain—Thomas Jenckes.
Lieutenant—Samuel Day.
Ensign—George Streeter.

SECOND COMPANY.

Captain—David Eddy.
Lieutenant—Ebenezer Trask.
Ensign—Simeon Ballou.

THIRD COMPANY.

Captain—Nehemiah Smith.
Lieutenant—James Smith.
Ensign—Jesse Smith.

The Smithfield and Cumberland Rangers were incorporated as an Independent Company. The company having chosen, the General Assembly appointed the following officers:

Captain—George Peck.
First Lieutenant—Nedibiah Wilkinson.
Second Lieutenant—Edward Thompson.
Ensign—Levi Brown.

All male persons, inhabitants of the Colony were required to subscribe, if required, the following "Declaration or Test:"

I the subscriber do solemnly and sincerely declare; That I believe the War, Resistance and Opposition in which the United American Colonies are now engaged against the fleets and armies of Great Britain, is on the part of the said Colonies just and necessary: And that I will not, directly, nor indirectly, afford assistance of any sort or kind whatever to the said fleets and armies, during the continuance of the present war; but that I will heartily assist in the defence of the United Colonies.

Provided: That in case any person shall produce a certificate from the Clerk of any Meeting of the Friends, that he is in Unity with that Society, or shall take the affirmation directed in an Act intituled "An Act for the Relief of Persons of tender Consciences, and for preventing their being burdened with military Duty," he shall be excused from subscribing the said Declaration or Test.

A Regiment of six hundred men was ordered to be raised; composed of six men out of every hundred, of sixteen years of age, and upwards. John Sayles, Jr., was chosen Colonel.

Daniel Mowry, Jr., was appointed, he being then at Newport, attending the General Assembly, to go immediately to the County of Providence, and make diligent enquiry after the persons concerned in counterfeiting the Bills of Credit emitted by this Colony.

1777. In January, 1777, the Smithfield and Cumberland Rangers, were upon their own application, ordered upon duty for three months. One-half of each company at a time. Thomas Appleby was permitted to take the place of his father James Appleby, Jr., who had been drafted.

David Wilkinson, Esq., was permitted to remove two barrels of rum from Smithfield to Providence.

Gideon Comstock was one of the Council of War to act during the recess of the General Assembly.

Gideon Comstock was appointed one of a committee to meet with any committee to be appointed by Massachusetts, to enquire into the grounds of the miscarriage of the late expedition against the enemy on Rhode Island.

Smithfield was required to furnish sixty-four pairs of stockings.

Daniel Mowry, Jr., was allowed fourteen pounds, five shillings, lawful money, for three days provision of thirty men who marched from the town of Smithfield.

Elisha Mowry appointed Lieut. Colonel of 2d Regiment.

The valuation of Smithfield was one hundred and eight thousand, seven hundred and eighty-five pounds; being the largest valuation of any country town save South Kingstown.

Jonathan Arnold, Henry Ward and Daniel Mowry were appointed a committee to revise, alter and amend an act for the relief of tender consciences.

April. Capt. Andrew Waterman was a committee to procure blankets.

May. Elisha Mowry was appointed Lieut. Colonel of the second regiment of Militia in Providence County.

Five hundred blankets, two hundred and fifty barrels of flour and eighty hundred weight of iron were ordered to be procured, and the proportion of each assessed to Smithfield, was: Sixteen barrels of flour, thirty-two blankets, and five hundred weight of iron.

Samuel Winsor was appointed to procure the blankets.

August.   John Angell and Peleg Arnold were appointed recruiting officers.

December.   Smithfield was required to furnish one hundred and twenty-eight pairs of stockings.

1778.   John Sayles was empowered to draw three hundred dollars out of the General Treasury in order to supply the families of the officers and soldiers in the town of Smithfield with necessaries.

Daniel Mowry, Jr., was appointed to inspect all letters that shall be received or sent by the late Capt. of the Syren, and to stop all such as he shall think improper to be delivered.

A new Council of War was appointed, of which Gideon Comstock was a member.   He was also one of a committee appointed to enquire into the matter of the defrauding of the State, by certain persons taking stock from the farm at Point Judith.

Valentine Whitman was permitted to transport " by land " to Boston, fifty or sixty hogsheads of tobacco, for the use of the United States.   But he was directed to appear before the General Assembly, to answer such questions as may be asked him, "respecting a quantity of cheese by him purchased in this State."

Peleg Arnold was one of a committee appointed by the General Assembly, to examine the clothing returned into the agent—clothiers store, for the use of the troops.

For the more equal representation of the State in the Council of War, a new Council was appointed by the General Assembly, of which Gideon Comstock and John Sayles were members.

John Sayles was allowed by the Council of War the sum of three hundred pounds lawful money in order to supply the families in the town of Smithfield, of soldiers in the Continental service.

Congress having recommended to the legislatures of the several States, to cause subscriptions to be opened for loans to the Continental service, the General Assembly appointed persons in the several sections of the State for that purpose; one of said persons being John Sayles.

The officers of the First Company of Militia were:

> Captain—Samuel Day.
> Lieutenant—Richard Sayles.
> Ensign—William Gully.

> SECOND COMPANY.

> Captain—Ebenezer Trask.
> Lieutenant—Simeon Ballou.
> Ensign—David Aldrich.

> THIRD COMPANY.

> Captain—Joseph Sprague.
> Fourth Lieutenant—Daniel Mowry.
> Ensign—Benjamin Sheldon.

John Sayles was appointed by the General Assembly to pay the bounties of soldiers enlisted in Smithfield, and this town was required to furnish fifty-one men.

Requisition was made upon Smithfield for 192 pair woolen stockings.

May. John Sayles and Gideon Comstock were appointed members of the Council of War.

October. William Aldrich was permitted, under the direction of General Sullivan, to go to England with Jemima Wilkinson.

A lottery to raise three hundred pounds, lawful money, was authorized, to repair the bridge over Pawtucket river near Unity Furnace, so called; now Manville.

The enlisting of men continued in 1778; and the town borrowed one thousand, seven hundred and eighty-five pounds for the purpose of paying bounties. The bounty had now been raised to thirty-five pounds, lawful money, in addition to the State's bounty, which was twenty pounds, with uniform. The drafted men who were to serve with Gen. Sullivan on the island of Rhode Island, were to be paid eighteen shillings per day. At this time it cost the town two pounds to enlist a man. The General Assembly having assessed the town in the number of one hundred and ninety-two pairs of woolen stockings, at the price of one pound and four shillings per pair; and the town being unable to procure them at that price, it was voted to collect them at the rate of forty shillings per pair, the town paying the difference.

At a special town meeting held on the second day of April, 1779, the following resolution was passed:

" Whereas upon the inspection of the prox proposed to be exhibited unto the several towns for electing General Officers, and Delegates to Congress for the year ensuing, give a general dissatisfaction to the people in this town; Whereupon it is unanimously voted, that Capt. Andrew Waterman, be and hereby is appointed a committee-man to meet such committee-men as may be appointed by our neighboring towns in this State, at East Greenwich, on the sixteenth day of this instant April, there in conjunction, as a committee, to select the best set of men they can engage for, to supply our righteous representation both in General Assembly, and General Congress, most for the utility of the State in particular, and the United States in general."

In 1779, Capt. Andrew Waterman was chosen to open a subscription to collect money to supply the town officer with the town's quota of money called for by Congress. Caleb Aldrich was sent to the Convention at East Greenwich, held for the purpose of further stipulating prices. In 1780, thirty-five more men were directed to be enlisted, and Col. John Sayles, Capt. William Waterman, Capt. Stephen Whipple and Capt. Hezekiah Sprague, were appointed a committee to hire 1750 silver dollars upon their personal security, and a tax of six hundred pounds was levied "in silver or gold," to be paid within four months. Caleb Aldrich, Esq., and Capt. Arnold Paine were chosen a committee to purchase the town's proportion of grain and beef, for the supply of the Commissary General. Three shillings in silver money was now paid by the town for each pair of woolen stockings, over and above what the State allowed, and thirty-five pairs were ordered bought. At this time began the enlistments for three years, or during the war, as also the collection of blankets for the soldiers.

The General Assembly having assessed the town for forty-two cwt. of beef, the town proposed to hire eighty-four pounds in hard money, to pay in lieu thereof: and the town voted to pay Stephen Whipple seventy-two old Continental Dollars in lieu of one silver dollar, in payment of this account. Eighty-three bushels of corn for the army, was ordered to be bought. In August, 1781, the town provided for twenty-seven bushels of corn, and 8026 lbs. beef for the months of October and November succeeding.

1779. February. The Deputy Governor, Gideon Comstock, Daniel Mowry and Rowse J. Helme were appointed a committee to take evidence concerning the illicit commerce carried on from the main to Block Island.

The committee was continued with power to apprehend and commit such persons as they thought proper. Daniel Mowry was appointed one of a committee to take an estimate of the ratable property in the State.

May. John Angell was appointed Lieut. Colonel of the second regiment of militia in the county of Providence.

Of the three militia companies in Smithfield, Eber Angell, Ebenezer Trask and Daniel Mowry, 4th, were Captains. Job Mowry was Captain of the Alarm Company.

October. Gideon Comstock, chosen a member of the Council of War.

Capt. Andrew Waterman, Jonathan Comstock, Esq., and Capt. William Potter were chosen delegates to meet delegates from the other towns in this State, to restore the Continental currency. Major Edward Thompson was afterwards put in place of Jonathan Comstock.

Samuel Winsor was allowed by the Council of War, seventeen pounds, ten shillings, ten pence, for articles supplied the family of Jonathan Hoight, belonging to the town of Smithfield.

The town council of Smithfield was allowed, by the Council of War, ninety dollars, for Thomas Herendeen, the same amount to Benjamin Smith, and to Stephen Gully. Being eighty-one pounds in lawful money.

Daniel Mowry was one of a committee appointed by the General Assembly, to prepare a bill in amendment to the act for the better supply of the army. Also to take an estimate of the ratable property in this State ; and to assess tax.

At a town meeting held in Smithfield on the 20th of August, 1779, called by Warrant, it was Voted: That we give our instruction to our Deputies to use their influence at the General Assembly, that this State's proportion of the twenty millions of dollars be raised.

That this town approves of the proceedings of the Convention met at East Greenwich, on the 10th of August, 1779, on stipulating prices of necessaries of life, &c.

That Caleb Aldrich,. Esq., Col. William Winsor and Capt. Stephen Whipple, be a committee to stipulate prices together with other committees in this county at time and place hereafter stipulated by the committee of Providence.

1780. March. John Sayles, Chairman, and others made report relative to the ways and means for procuring supplies for the Continental Army. Sylvanus Sayles, Chairman, and others were empowered to procure a sufficient quantity of linen to be manufactured to make ninety pairs of breeches for the officers in the Continental Army, considered to be the quota of this State.

June. William Aldrich was appointed Major of the second regiment of militia, in the County of Providence. Peleg Arnold, Lieutenant Colonel Commandant, of the second Battalion, in the County of Providence.

Smithfield required to furnish thirty-five men for the Continental Battalions.

Uriah Alverson to receive the money to pay bounties.

Elisha Mowry, Jr., appointed to procure blankets in Smithfield.

July. The General Assembly directed that the Continental Army be supplied, in each month of July, August, September and October, with 71,675 pounds of beef, and 2,285 bushels of corn, rye, oats or barley; and the monthly quota of Smithfield was 5,000 pounds of beef, and 150 bushels of grain.

The ratable polls in town, were 425; the amount of money and trading stock, 2,143 pounds; ounces of plate, 1,157; horses, 346; oxen, 413; horned cattle, 2,370; sheep and goats, 3,449; amount of the ratable value, 194,864 pounds. In November, however, a revision was made of this estimate, and Smithfield was rated for 212,509.01 pounds; and again at the same session the rate was finally fixed at 207,809.01 pounds.

There was a deficiency of 163 men in the quotas ordered to be raised in June, but Smithfield had much more nearly raised her proportion than had some of the towns in the southern part of the State. Six hundred and thirty more men were ordered to be raised, and Smithfield was required to furnish thirty-five. Peleg Arnold, John Sayles, John Angell, Andrew Waterman, Stephen Whipple, Ebenezer Trask and Edward Thompson were appointed recruiting officers.

Rufus Streeter was appointed Ensign of the first company in the militia in the town of Smithfield. The following officers having been chosen by the company, were appointed by the Council of War, for the Smithfield and Cumberland Rangers, to wit:

> Captain—Edward Thompson.
> First Lieutenant—Benjamin Walcot.
> Second Lieutenant—William Bowen.
> Ensign—Joshua Jenckes.

George Streeter was appointed Lieutenant in the senior class in Smithfield; and Abraham Winsor, Ensign.

This town was assessed to furnish, as its quota for one month five thousand pounds of beef, and one hundred and fifty bushels of grain, being a larger amount of beef than that assessed upon any town save South Kingstown. Elisha Mowry, Jr., was appointed to assist in collecting the same in this town.

In October, requisition was made upon Smithfield for twelve blankets, and thirty-five pairs of stockings, being more than was required of Newport, and nearly the same quantity as was asked of Providence. The blankets were to cost not over eighty pounds lawful money, each, for the best; and the best quality of stockings not over twelve pounds per pair. If they could not be purchased, the col lectors were empowered to take them by distraint.

Peleg Arnold was chosen Lieutenant-Colonel, commandant of the second Battalion, in the County of Providence.

Peleg Arnold, John Sayles, John Angell, Andrew Waterman, Stephen Whipple, Ebenezer Trask and Edward Thompson were a committee to receive recruits; and Smithfield was required to furnish thirty-five men.

Daniel Mowry was elected Delegate to Congress.

November. John Jenckes was appointed one of a com mittee " to inspect into the public letters and papers laid before this Assembly."

The number of acres in town was estimated to be 35,236; the value per acre five pounds, ten shillings; value of real estate, 193,798 pounds; total value, 212,509 pounds.

The valuation was slightly reduced upon revisal.

One hundred and twenty pounds found due to Elisha Mowry for blankets bought.

1781. February. Twelve hundred men were ordered into service for one month. Daniel Mowry, 4th., Captain in the Battalion of Providence and Kent Counties.

William Waterman, appointed to purchase corn for the army, for the town of Smithfield.

May. Daniel Mowry, 4th, Major of second regiment of militia in the County of Providence.

Job Mowry, Captain in the Second Battalion.

Benjamin Ballou, Ebenezer Trask and John Carpenter, Captains.

July. William Waterman, for Smithfield, was directed to furnish twenty-seven bushels of grain for the army.

August. The same number of bushels were directed to be furnished for September, October and November.

A requisition was made upon Smithfield for twenty-seven bushels of corn or rye. Providence was required to furnish twenty-nine bushels, and South Kingstown, forty.

In 1781, Daniel Mowry, 4th, Esq., was Major of the second regiment of militia in the County of Providence.

In 1782, the ratable value of Smithfield was put at two hundred thousand pounds.

The population of the town was 2,217.

1783. At a town meeting held June 2, 1783, it was voted:

"We the inhabitants of the town of Smithfield, in town meeting assembled, being impressed with a sense of the iniquity and inhumanity of the practice of enslaving the human species, and being

fully convinced of this standing truth that all men are born to an
equal right of liberty; and while we are contending for the inestimable privilege ourselves, to be acting the tyrant over, and bringing
others into abject slavery is as great an inconsistency as a rational
being can be guilty of, and sufficiently evinces that such people are
only craving it for themselves for their own enjoyment without pos-
sessing the spirit of liberty in their own minds: Therefore we instruct
and direct you our Representatives to use your endeavors and influence
in the General Assembly, to procure a law made and passed that no
ship or vessel shall be fitted out from any part of this State to Africa,
unless the Master or Captain thereof shall give bonds in such a sum,
and be under such lawfull restrictions, regulations and obligations as
the legislative body shall seem suitable, and deem effective to debar
him from purchasing or bringing away from the country the inhabitants, and making slaves of them, or selling them for slaves in any of
the West India Islands or elsewhere."

1784.   Daniel Mowry, Jr., was chosen delegate, and Gideon Comstock and John Sayles, a committee to consider and
instruct said delegate in relation to the inequality of the State
representation in the General Assembly, in view of a convention.

1786.   WE THE FREEMEN OF THE TOWN OF SMITHFIELD, assembled in legal town meeting to make choice of Deputies to represent us
in the General Assembly at next May session, and to put in our proxy
votes for general officers, being seriously and weightily concerned for
the good people of this State, and for those of this town in particular,
of which we have complete knowledge, of the difficulties and oppres-
sions they live under.

For that there hath been several heavy and unjust taxes brought on,
assessed and collected by order of the legislators of this State, and the
money appropriated to them where it was not one-half due.   It hath
been raised, as it is said, to pay the interest of the money put into the
Loan Office, and to those that are the holders of other public securities,
when the money loaned did not pass, and was not worth one-quarter,
and some not more than twenty for one in silver money.   And many
of the public securities originated from as small a value.   The certificates were given for paper money, which was then called lawful
money, and have not been liquidated to the just value.   So there
have been many examples where one year's interest hath been paid in

silver, that was worth more than the principal was, when loaned. And at this time there is another tax of twenty thousand pounds ordered and assessed on this little and oppressed State and ordered to be appropriated in an unjust manner as the former, which ought never to be collected or paid. And to our great surprise and astonishment, the legislators of this State, in one of their late sessions, complied with the requisition of Congress, 'wherein was contained the paying of the interest of the loaned money on the principal sum loaned, though they acknowledge it is subject to a liquidation.

And also did pass an act called an act giving and granting to the United States in Congress assembled, an impost of five per cent. on all foreign goods imported into this State, for the space of twenty-five years, to be collected by a Congress officer who is demeanable to none living but Congress, and it is said to be applied to pay the interest and principal of any of the expenses incurred by the late war. And as there is none to call Congress to account for the expenditures, on earth, it is in their hands, at their uncontrolled will. If the legislature think it best to raise money by impost, we have not a word to say against it. And at the same time we are sensible it is raised out of the consumer of the goods. But we are of opinion, on principles well founded, that it ought to be collected by officers of the State, and deposited in the general treasury and disposed of by the General Assembly. If the cause of the impost being granted at this time and after this manner, may appear a mystery, but about three years ago Congress insisted earnestly for the same measures and employed several gentlemen, one of which was Mr. Paine, a great writer in favor of liberty, to attend our Assembly, to enforce same. But all to no purpose, for the Assembly, sincerely and manfully opposed it, as being impolitic, unconstitutional and unjust, and giving up the rights and interests of the State, which was generally acknowledged by some of the other States to be to their great honor, and also to the honor of the State they represented, and had a good effect in the other States that had in some degree complied with the measure, who soon repealed the same. And what the cause is now, we do not pretend to affirm; but we think it favors the story of paying the interest and principal of the loaned money agreeable to the face of the certificates without liquidation. These proceedings we think to be grievances of a high nature, and not only think them so, but we feel them so, and that the same in truth and good conscience ought to be redressed, and in order thereto, we in the early part of this meeting, before our representatives are elected, do give the following instructions to those

7

that may be chosen, that they may know the sense of this town at their acceptance of that important trust.

1st.   Whereupon, our advice and instructions to you, gentlemen, are, that you attend the General Assembly at their several sittings for May session; that you use your utmost endeavors and influence to stop and hinder any more money being paid in this State, either by taxes, impost, or any other way, for interest or principal on Loan Office certificates, or any public securities, subject to a liquidation, till the just value they originated from is known and the same be reduced thereto; and where the full value is paid on any of the securities, that it be so declared and the same cancelled; and if more be paid on any, than what is right and equitable, that strict justice may be done.

2d.   That you use your utmost endeavors and exert yourselves in debates and in voting, to procure that part of an act, called "An Act granting an impost of five per cent. to the United States in Congress assembled, on all foreign goods imported into this State," to be repealed, so far as relates to Congress, or to the officer that collects the same being a Congress officer or demeanable to Congress; and that the General Assembly fill up and finish that part of the act which they left Congress to do.   And that the collector or collectors be accountable to the General Treasurer, and the money arising on the impost be deposited in the general treasury and disposed by the General Assembly.

3d.   That you move it in the General Assembly that proper means be used and applications made that the accounts with the United States be settled, and that this State may know what we have to pay and what we pay it for, and that we pay it our own way.   And that you do not order any money to be paid for the United States' debts till this be done, for it is of the uttermost bad consequence to lie, as it doth, and may save the trouble of many requisitions being sent.

4th.   That you move once more, that a more equal representation be had in this State, and if not obtained, we think we ought to be and are exonerated from paying any more taxes till done.

In town meeting at Smithfield, April 19th, 1786.   The within requisitions were read and debated in town meeting, and voted to be given as instructions to the representatives of this town in General Assembly, at the May session next.

Witness,   DANIEL MOWRY, *Town Clerk.*

At a special town meeting held October 21, 1786, it was voted that the town does not approve of an act forwarded from the General Assembly, intended to stimulate and give efficacy to the paper bills emitted by this State; and George Comstock, Daniel Mowry, Jr., Esq., Thomas Lapham, Gideon Comstock, Esq., and Elisha Bartlett were appointed a committee to draft instructions for the Representatives in that behalf. In December of this year a committee was chosen to inspect into the state and circumstances of the poor. April, 1787, the Deputies were instructed to endeavor to procure the passage of a law giving the towns a more equal representation in the General Assembly. In March, 1788, the town voted 159 to 2 against the proposed Constitution; and also in favor of the repeal of the paper money tender act. In 1798 the town for the first time provided for the keeping of the poor, by vendue; they being put out for the year to the lowest bidder. If this seems, in this day a harsh and unfeeling mode of caring for the unfortunate, a glance at the conditions of the contract and the safeguards thrown around the welfare of the poor, will relieve the natural but unjust suspicion. The poor were to be clothed, fed, lodged, nursed in sickness and provided "with all such necessaries fitting for them in their degree." Two or more of the overseers of the poor were to visit them as often as once in two months, to see if they were decently kept and provided for; and if complaint be made, oftener, if they think necessary. At the August meeting, 1799, upon consideration of an act passed by the General Assembly to establish free schools, it was thought that the terms of said act were more peculiarly adapted to the interests of the sea-port and compact towns than to those of the country towns, and Philip Mowry, William Buffum, Joel Aldrich, Elisha Olney, Duty Winsor, Edward Medbury and John Jenckes, 3d, were appointed a committee "to examine every paragraph and article therein, and upon mature investigation to report their opinion and judgment in relation thereto; whether for the best to adopt or reject."

At the September meeting, the said committee reported in favor of the adoption of said school act, and the town accepted said report, and instructed the Representatives to endeavor to have said act passed into a law. In June, 1800, William Buffum, Joel Aldrich, Ezekiel Comstock, Thomas Mann, Elisha Olney, Robert Harris, Thomas Appleby, Jonathan Harris and Joseph Farnum were chosen a committee "in order to provide ways and means to organize and prescribe the best plan to put in motion the Free School Act; and proportion off, how many schools are necessary, and where to be kept for the convenience of the town of Smithfield——who have engaged to set and consult the premises without cost to the town." At the August town meeting, the said committee reported that they had agreed upon twenty-six as the number of schools; a tax of one thousand dollars was voted to be levied for the support thereof.

April, 1801, the price of a day's work on the highway was raised to seventy-five cents, fifty per cent. advance. At this time a special town meeting could be called upon request of seven freemen, and as the General Assembly had passed an act requiring in such cases formal notice to the freemen, the town, having under said law the right to prescribe for itself, the mode of calling such special meetings, Voted, that they should be called by posting notices in five public places, and designated such places as follows: at Peleg Arnold's; at Sylvanus Bucklin's; at Scott Pond Halls; at Robert Harris's; and upon the great road at Tucker and Sevours. All these designated places were then public houses. April, 1805, the overseers of the poor were directed to bind out to proper persons the children, from the age of four years and upwards, being poor of the town. At the annual town meeting in June, 1806, the Representatives to the General Assembly were instructed to use their endeavors, at the next and all future Assemblys to cause resolutions to be passed, recommending the people to give their suffrages either in favor of, or against a convention of delegates, for the purpose of forming a Constitution for this State.

At a Convention of members from all the towns in the County of Providence, met at Smithfield, on the 13 day of September, 1781; Gideon Comstock Esq., was chosen chairman, and John Harris Esq., clerk. Voted: That a committee be appointed to draught some recommendations, to lay before the several towns for their approbation, and that they instruct their Deputies accordingly. Voted: That Benoni Williams, Sylvanus Sayles, Hon. William West, Rev. Philemon Hines, Joab Young, Roger Sheldon, Nehemiah Atwood, Stephen Olney and Jonathan Hopkins be the committee. The report of the committee recited, that: "Whereas it appears that the distress of the good people of this State is truly alarming, on account of the unstable state of the paper currency, the instability of which arises from the opposition of the mercantile interest within this State: And whereas it is evident that great profit ariseth from importation; and also that for our produce we can import silver or gold, which we must have to discharge our foreign debt and foreign expenses, which we have been prevented doing by the exportation of cash; and also considering it to be good policy for any State to make use of every advantage in their power to extricate themselves from every embarrassment under which they may labor; and that it is their duty to support their inhabitants with the conveniences of life as far as possible: We the committee recommend to the inhabitants of this State that they call town meetings, and instruct their Deputies to use their influence at the next General Assembly to form a State-Trade; and that they provide vessels for that purpose; and that the taxes that are assessed, by order of Assembly, which is not otherwise appropriated, to be appropriated for the purposes aforesaid, and the proceeds be appropriated to supply the said inhabitants, and to discharge our foreign debt and expenses as aforesaid; which business shall be transacted under the General Assembly, or those that they shall appoint for that purpose. Also that they instruct their Deputies to use their utmost efforts to obtain a repeal of that statute which introduces the law making notes of hand negotiable in this State; and that the statute of limitations be shortened to two years from the rising of the said Assembly. And also that the General Treasurer be directed to issue no more interest certificates receivable by the Collectors of Impost, but that the importers pay the Collectors in money. And also that an excise on the superfluities and luxuries of life, be properly established, and punctually executed. Also we recommend to the inhabitants of this State that they keep on hand all those articles which are most suitable for exportation, until a full determination can be had on the aforesaid recommendation by the General Assembly ; and that the collection of taxes for the purposes aforesaid be in the following manner, viz: in Money, Produce, Lumber, or Labor, at stipulated prices, for carrying the aforesaid State-Trade into effect."

A call was made in form upon the Governor, to call the General Assembly together "as soon as can be convenient."

1786.. February. A lottery was granted to raise four hundred and fifty dollars for the repair of the bridge near Unity Furnace, Jotham Carpenter Esq., of Cumberland, and Capt. David Sayles, of Smithfield, managers.

1787. During the session of the Continental Congress, in this year, at New York, there was published in the *Daily . Advertiser*, of that city, an article headed: " Quintessence of villany ; or, proceedings of the Legislature of the State of Rhode Island at the late session." Which article was construed to be a " daring insult to a sovereign State, by our Representatives, James M. Varnum and Peleg Arnold."

A letter was addressed by them to the Governor of the State of New York, requesting him to cause the publisher of said paper to be apprehended for publishing said libel. The Legislature of New York ordered the prosecution of the printer, if our delegates should request; but they deemed their views to have been fully met, and declined to have the prosecution entered upon. Their point was to sustain the honor of the State.

1788. At the March session of the General Assembly, a motion was made in the House of Representatives for a Convention to act upon the adoption of the Constitution framed at Philadelphia as and for the Constitution of the United States. It was negatived by twenty-seven majority, as the same motion had been negatived by a majority of thirty at a previous session. In June, nine States had adopted the Constitution, and it became apparent that it would eventually receive the assent of all the States. The citizens of Providence who were largely in favor of the new national government, at a public meeting resolved to celebrate " the adoption of the Federal Constitution by nine States," and the anniversary of American Independence, on the Fourth of July. The celebration " was to be on the plain to the northward of the bay or cove." In the newspapers was inserted a general invitation to the town and country to assemble on this occasion, and special invitations were issued to the State officials. " The public at large," says Judge West, " seeing preparations for so public a celebration of the adoption of the same Constitution, which had already received the disapprobation and disgust of at least four-fifths of the individual inhabitants of this State, as well as of the legislative authority of the State, did thereupon at once perceive, that such entertainment in such public manner, was intended as a public insult upon the legislative authority of the State as well as the body of the peo-

ple at large." The celebration of Independence as a part
of said festival was considered to be a mockery, a delusion
and a snare to the country people. Whereupon it was determined to prevent the celebration of the intended feast
for which great preparation was making, and at which
there was to be an ox roasted whole. During the night of
the third of July about one thousand men from all the
surrounding country assembled under arms, and there was
every prospect of the attendance of two or three times that
number before noon on the Fourth. About eleven o'clock
of the night of the third, the town sent a committee to enquire what the country demanded, whereupon they were
informed, that the country had no objection to the celebration of any occasion, except that of the new Constitution,
or its adoption by any of the States, on which it was agreed
that a committee of each party should meet in the morning
with an endeavor to accommodate matters to the satisfaction of the country.

The committee from the town consisted of Jabez Bowen,
David Howell, Welcome Arnold, John I. Clark, Benjamin
Bourne, Esqs., Col. Zephaniah Andrews, and Mr. John
Mason. The committee of the country consisted of William
West, Esq., Capt. Andrew Waterman, Abraham Mathewson,
John Westcott, and Peleg Fisk, Esqs., Col. John Sayles and
Capt. James Aldrich.

After a conference of about an hour, it was agreed on the
part of the town, that they would not celebrate the day on
account of the adoption of the Constitution by nine States, or
on account of said Constitution, in any respect whatever;
that no salutes should be fired or toasts drank in honor of
said Constitution, or in honor of any State or States which
have adopted said Constitution, that they would only honor
the day by a discharge of thirteen cannon and thirteen only,
that the celebration of the day should be in honor of the
independence of America, and that only, and that they would

not publish or cause to be published any account contrary
to said agreement.   One member from each committee went
to the troops under arms and declared to them the particu-
lars of the aforesaid agreement; whereupon they retired in
pursuance of said agreement.

1790. January.   The General Treasurer laid before the
Assembly the deficiency of the several towns in the payment
of the tax assessed at the June session, 1788, and it appeared
that the sums unpaid varied from over one thousand pounds,
to one pound.   Smithfield was deficient only two pounds
eight shillings and seven pence.

At a Convention of Delegates, begun and holden at South
Kingstown, in the County of Washington, on the first Monday
in March, 1790, pursuant to an act of the General Assembly,
passed at their session in January, 1790, for the purpose of
investigating and deciding on the new Constitution, proposed
for the United States: John Sayles, Esq., and Andrew
Waterman, Esq., were delegates from Smithfield.   Mr.
Waterman was one of the committee to prepare Rules and
Orders for the government of the Convention.   Col. Sayles
moved that a committee be appointed to form a bill of
rights and prepare amendments to the proposed Constitution, formed by the Convention at Philadelphia, on the 17th
day of September, 1787, for the government of the United
States, and report to the Convention, and that the Convention do adjourn to a future day.   Seconded by Andrew
Waterman.   Laid upon the table.   Upon motion afterwards
made a committee was appointed, consisting of two from
each county, to draft amendments to be proposed to the
new Federal Constitution.   The members for the county of
Providence, were, Stephen Steere, Esq., and John Sayles,
Esq.   On motion of Andrew Waterman the Convention adjourned to the fourth Monday in May, at Newport.   Upon
the question of adopting "the federal government," the vote

8

was thirty-four in the affirmative, and thirty-two in the negative, the delegates from Smithfield voting in the negative.

An Act to incorporate certain persons by the name of the " Providence Society for promoting the abolition of Slavery, for the relief of persons unlawfully held in bondage, and for improving the condition of the African race," was passed by the General Assembly.   Among the persons named in the act, were the following, of Smithfield: Arnold Paine, John Sayles, and Peleg Arnold.   Among the corporators, was Jonathan Edwards, of Connecticut.

1791.   The "Smithfield Grenadiers" chartered, comprising the following persons: Samuel McClellan, John Jenckes, Jr., William Harris, William Arnold, Jr., Richard Angel, John Angel, Jr., Isaac Angel, Thomas Angel, Charles Angel, Jr., Benjamin Angell, John Arnold, Thomas Arnold, William Aldrich, Jr., Daniel Arnold, Jr., Smith Arnold, Job Angel, Jr., James Bryant, William Bryant, Stephen Brayton, Jr., William Ballou, Nicholas Brock, William Dexter, James Drake, Jacob File, William Gray, Benjamin Harris, Uriah Harris, Job Harris, Nicholas Jenckes, George Jenckes, David Jenckes, Daniel Jenckes, Benjamin Jenckes, William Legg, Jonathan Lapham, Ahab Mowry, Nathaniel Mowry, Daniel Olney, Zelotus Olney, Loammi Tucker, Joseph Tucker, Henry Sprague, Joseph Sprague, Jr., Simeon Wilkinson, John Wilkinson, Jr., Joseph Wilkinson, Arnold Whipple, Jeremiah Whipple, John White, Jesse Whipple, Nathan Young, Samuel Thayer and Samuel Mann.

The officers were:

Captain—Samuel McClellan.
First Lieutenant—Zenas Winsor.
Second Lieutenant—John Jenckes, Jr.
Ensign—William Harris.

June.   A tax of six thousand pounds, lawful money, was

assessed.   Smithfield to pay three hundred and eighty-six pounds.

1792.   At the February session the General Assembly enacted: Whereas the preservation of this State, as well as of other States, depends, under the protection of God, upon the military skill and discipline of the inhabitants; and whereas a number of the inhabitants of the town of Smithfield, to wit: Zenas Winsor, Joab Mathewson, Peleg Peck, Job Aldrich, Jr., Olney Latham, Daniel Tinkom, William Newell, Elisha Latham, Ichabod Potter, Constant Luther, William Moffiatt, John Russell, Jeremiah Winsor, Jr., William Potter, Jr., William Potter, 3d, Christopher Wilkinson, Samuel Weston, Elijah Day, John Crosby, Abraham Mathewson, Jr., Josiah Deane, Benajah Dyse, Oliver Jenckes, Stephen Sprague, Charles Salisbury, Edward Pike, William Hicks, Amos Eddy, John Slocum, Asher Saunders, George Smith, Joseph Mathewson, Thomas Dyer, James Sweet, Nathaniel Thatcher, Hendrick Smith, Elisha Evans, Emor Olney, Philip Keach, Joseph Carpenter, Solomon Paine, Oliver Saunders, Daniel Winsor, Pardon Smith, Andrew Waterman, Jr., Joseph Mitchell, Noah Bartlett, Jr., Juni Smith, David Comstock, Christopher Smith, Gardner Aldrich, Simeon Potter, Barlow Aldrich, William Shumway, Benjamin Waterman, John Appleby, David Tucker, James Brown, George Aldrich, Nathaniel Mowry, Jr., Daniel Aldrich, Daniel Tucker, Joseph Aldrich, Thomas Steere, Jabez Mowry, Caleb Shrieve, Nathaniel Mowry, 3d, Samuel Mowry, Stephen Appleby, and James Appleby, of Smithfield, in the County of Providence, have offered to form a company by the name of the Federal Protectors: Wherefore, this General Assembly, in order to give due encouragement to so laudable a design, have ordained, constituted and granted * * * that said petitioners be an independent company.

The officers were:

Captain—Zenas Winsor.
First Lieutenant—Joab Mathewson.
Second Lieutenant—Peleg Peck.
Ensign—Job Aldrich, Jr.

February.   Daniel Mowry was appointed one of the commissioners upon the boundary line between this State and
Massachusetts.

October.   John Sayles appointed to collect, in the County
of Providence, the money due upon the bonds taken for the
interest of the bills of credit emitted May, 1786.

Caleb Aldrich appointed one of a committee to report
upon the removal of certain obstructions to the passage of
fish up Pawtucket river.

At the February session of the General Assembly, 1797,
Joshua Jenckes, Joseph Wilkinson, Simeon Wilkinson, Na-
than Dexter, Christopher Dexter, Ahab Mowry, Benjamin
Ballou, Jr., Jesse Mowry, Charles Wright, Joseph Hendrick,
Winsor Aldrich, Rufus Streeter, Jeremiah Newman, Samuel
Clarke, Nathaniel Mowry, William Mowry, Jesse Whipple,
Nahum Aldrich, George Harris, Simon Whipple, Job Page,
Stephen Clarke, Sally Page, Amos Lapham, Adam Jenckes,
William Jenckes, George Eddy, Peter Harris, Samuel Mann,
Nathaniel Streeter, William Harris, George Hill, John Jenckes,
Jr., Isaac Comstock, Nicholas Jenckes, Lewis Dexter, Charles
Angell, Jr., Edward Tripp, James Bryan, Jonathan Harris,
Simon Harris, Thomas Mann, Benjamin Newell, Jesse Harris,
George Streeter, Dexter Ballou, Smith Sayles, Welcome Har-
ris, George Chace, Jonathan Lapham, Nathaniel Spaulding,
William Aldrich, Jr., and Job Lapham, were made a "Body
politic and corporate by the name of the Smithfield Third
Library-Company."

The purpose was to establish a library of useful books,
certain of the incorporated members having theretofore
associated themselves together for said purpose.   But the
corporation was authorized to hold lands to the value of five

thousand dollars. It will be seen at once over what a wide territory these persons were distributed, and how modest were their ideas as to the value of the "tenement" in which to place that library owned, or to be owned by so numerous a company, with right to admit others, and, in the language of the charter, "to subsist at all times forever hereafter."

1805. Joseph Farnum, Noah Farnum, Jabez Mowry, Stephen Olney, William F. Magee, Henry Smith, Fenner Angell, Nicholas Brown, Rufus Waterman, Amos T. Jenckes, George Weeden, James Smith, Noah Arnold, Benjamin Sheldon, David Mowry, Gardner Aldrich, Artemas Smith, Delvin Smith, Chad Smith, Cyrus Cook, Thomas Arnold, Eleazer Bellows, Richard Mowry, Enos Mowry and others were incorporated for the purpose of building and establishing a turnpike road from Providence to the line of Massachusetts in Douglass or Uxbridge.

The Smithfield Turnpike Company was incorporated at the February session of the General Assembly, 1805, the following named persons being the incorporators: Joseph Farnum, Noah Farnum, Jabez Mowry, Stephen Olney, William F. Magee, Henry Smith, Fenner Angell, Nicholas Brown, Rufus Waterman, Amos T. Jenckes, George Weeden, James Smith, Noah Arnold, Benjamin Sheldon, David Mowry, Gardner Aldrich, Artemas Smith, Delvin Smith, Chad Smith, Cyrus Cook, Thomas Arnold, Eleazer Bellows, Richard Mowry, and Enos Mowry.

February, 1805, the Smithfield Union Bank was incorporated with a capital of fifty thousand dollars, and, having been chosen by the stockholders, Peleg Arnold, Stephen Whipple, Enos Mowry, Baruch Aldrich, William Buffum, Duty Winsor, Jesse Brown, Walter Allen, Thomas Mann, Simon Whipple, Thomas Aldrich, Elisha Olney and Joel Aldrich were appointed temporary Directors.

August, 1807, the town voted to rebuild the middle bridge

at Woonsocket Falls, as had theretofore been done between
the towns of Smithfield and Cumberland; and at the same
time appropriated two hundred dollars toward rebuilding
the westernmost, or capital bridge at Woonsocket Falls.

1807. October. John Slater having petitioned therefor,
Seth Mowry, Robert Harris, Enos Mowry and Ananias Mowry were empowered to raise four thousand dollars by lottery, to be appropriated to building a meeting house in the
town of Smithfield.

1808. October. Samuel Clark, Simon Aldrich, Simon
Whipple, John Jenckes, 2d, Jeremiah Whipple, Ahab Mow-
ry, Nathaniel Mowry, Winsor Aldrich, James Aldrich and
Susannah Jenckes were incorporated by the name of the
Smithfield School Society, and empowered to hold property
to the amount of ten thousand dollars.

Enos Mowry, Ananias Mowry, Seth Mowry and Arnold
Mowry were empowered to raise the sum of two thousand
dollars by lottery, for the benefit of the Smithfield Academic
Society.

At the October session, 1808, the Smithfield Academic
Society was incorporated, Enos Mowry, Seth Mowry and
Nicholas Brown being incorporators.

1810. February. Peleg Arnold, Richard Steere, Ezekiel
Comstock, Joel Aldrich, John W. C. Baxter and David
Aldrich were made a body corporate by the name of The
Trustees of the Smithfield Academy. They were empow-
ered to hold real and personal property, not exceeding in
all, five thousand dollars.

President—Peleg Arnold.
Vice-President—Joel Aldrich.
Treasurer—Richard Steere.
Secretary—David Aldrich.

Peleg Arnold, Marcus Arnold and George Aldrich were

authorized to raise by lottery the sum of fifteen hundred dollars, for the erection of a building for the Smithfield Academy.

October. William Steere, David Sayles and John Esten made report to the General Assembly that they had expended more money in building a meeting house, than they had received from a lottery.

1812. February. Duty Winsor, Daniel Winsor, Anson Mowry, Elijah Day, Emor Olney, Nathan B. Sprague, Augustus Winsor, Jr., Ziba Smith, Abraham Smith and Asa Winsor incorporated as Trustees of the Greene Academy; to hold property to the amount of five thousand dollars.

A lottery was granted to the benefit of the Greene Academy.

February 12, 1812, the Trustees of the Greene Academy in Smithfield were incorporated. The incorporators were Duty Winsor, Daniel Winsor, Aaron Mowry, Elijah Day, Emor Olney, Nathan B. Sprague, Augustus Winsor, Jr., Ziba Smith, Abraham Smith, and Asa Winsor. And at the February session, 1812, the trustees were granted the right to hold a lottery to raise twenty-two hundred dollars.

June, 1812, the town considering that the sum of five dollars per month allowed by Congress to the soldiers drafted from the town was inadequate to common laborers; and feeling that the general complaint in regard thereto was just, voted that such drafted men, or any who should serve for them, should be paid by the town seven dollars per month.

1814. The Independent Smithfield Rifle Company was incorporated.

> Captain—Thomas Wright.
> First Lieutenant—Benjamin Bennett.
> Second Lieutenant—Jonathan Cole.
> Ensign—Benjamin Harris.

1814. The Smithfield Light Infantry Company was incorporated.

> Captain—Jedediah Carpenter.
> Lieutenant—Samuel Taft.
> Ensign—Henry Carpenter.

At the October session of the General Assembly, A. D. 1818, Thomas Buffum, David Ide, Rowland Rathbone, Winsor Aldrich, Nathaniel Mowry, 3d, Jeremiah Smith, William Buffum, Jr., Ezekiel Comstock and James Harkness were made a corporation by the name and style of the New England Pacific Bank, to be located and established in the town of Smithfield. The capital stock was fifty thousand dollars. The Directors, until others were elected, were named in the charter, as follows: Thomas Buffum, Nathaniel Mowry, 3d, William Buffum, Jr., Ezekiel Comstock and James Harkness.

1820. The first Cadet Company in the sixth Regiment of Militia was incorporated.

> Captain—Harris J. Mowry.
> First Lieutenant—Otis Marsh.
> Second Lieutenant—Simon Aldrich, 3d.
> Ensign—Charles C. Mowry.

August, 1821, it was voted to "cause a town house to be built in some convenient part of said town;" and Reuben Mowry, Thomas Mann and Thomas Buffum were chosen a committee to procure a lot, and build the town house.

1822. Joseph Wilkinson and Benjamin Coe were appointed a committee to ascertain the middle of the bridge at Woonsocket Falls, and repair the Smithfield half of the bridge or bridges. There was some dissatisfaction at the action of the committee in locating the town house on the town's lot "near the White School House," but it was voted that it should proceed to build there. The members of Congress were instructed to use their influence to get some alterations in the Bankrupt Bill, in agitation before Congress. The former action in relation to the town house was repealed. The bridge committee aforesaid, was directed to negotiate with the authorities of the town of Cumberland in relation to the bridges at Woonsocket, Unity (Manville) and " Whipple's." A survey of the town was also moved. It was voted 89 to 0 in favor of a written Constitution for this State.

June, 1822, Daniel Winsor, Daniel Mathewson, Jesse Foster and Stephen W. Smith were incorporated by the name of The Baptist Society in the southwesterly part of Smithfield.

June, 1822, Daniel Winsor, Joseph Mathewson, Dexter Irons, Nathan B. Sprague, Asa Winsor, Richard Smith, Stephen Steere, John S. Appleby, Reuben Mowry, Silas Smith and Elisha Steere were incorporated as The Smithfield Exchange Bank. Capital stock forty thousand dollars.

1823. Joseph Wilkinson was appointed to attend to the indictment against Cumberland in regard to the bridges at Woonsocket; Smithfield had been indicted in the same behalf, a few years before. A tax was voted to be levied upon the Blackstone Cotton factory, and thereafter the Representatives were instructed to oppose the petition of the Blackstone Manufacturing Company to the General Assembly, in relation to said tax.

October, 1824, it was voted 129 to 18 in favor of the Constitution framed at Newport, in June preceding.

October, 1826, the eastern and lower section of the Smithfield and Glocester Turnpike, was designated as the Mineral Spring Turnpike.

In 1827, the town voted that the Representatives in the General Assembly use their influence to procure a law taxing cotton and woolen machinery in the town where operated; and that they should endeavor to procure the repeal of the new Judiciary law. The northern line of the town was not

9

fairly established, and Thomas Mann and Joseph Wilkinson were appointed a committee to ascertain whether the new factory of Welcome and Darius Farnum was or not in Rhode Island.

January, 1828, Nathaniel Mowry, 2d, Winsor Aldrich, Simon Whipple, Ahab Mowry, Nathan Aldrich, John Dexter, Jesse Mowry, Nathaniel Scott, Jeremiah Smith, Amasa Mowry, Stephen G. Arnold, Sterry Jenckes, Jeremiah Whipple, George Smith and John Jenckes were incorporated by the name of the Smithfield Lime Rock Bank. Capital stock one hundred thousand dollars.

1828. Messrs. John Harris, Jr., of Scituate, Thomas Mann, of Smithfield, Samuel W. King, of Johnston, George Burton, of Cranston, Barney Merry, of North Providence, and Benjamin C. Harris, of Providence, were made a committee to superintend the drawing the Free Will Baptist Society's Lottery, in Smithfield.

1832. Samuel Greene, Joseph M. Brown, James Wilson, Jr., Ariel Ballou, Jr., Edward Harris, and others were incorporated by the name of the St. James Church, at Woonsocket Falls in Smithfield; and the corporation was authorized to hold property in the sum of fifty thousand dollars.

January, 1834, Lewis Dexter, Jeremiah Smith, Morton Mowry, and others were incorporated into a banking company, by the name of the President, Directors and Company of the Providence County Bank. The capital stock was fifty thousand dollars.

Location changed to Woonsocket, 1855. Name changed to Globe Bank.

In 1835, Arnold Spear and Lewis Dexter as a committee for the town, purchased the Seth Mowry farm for five thousand five hundred dollars; and in 1836, Ethan Harris was chosen to "repair the outside of the town's meeting house, and make some necessary repairs inside of said house."

1835. Timothy W. Dexter, and his associates, were incorporated by the name of Christ's Church in Lonsdale, in Smithfield; for the purpose of establishing and maintaining public worship. The corporation was authorized to hold property to the amount of thirty thousand dollars.

1836. Daniel Hale, Stephen P. Train, John Vannerar, Nathan Young, Bradbury C. Hill, Washington Wilkinson and others were incorporated by the name of Emanuel Church, at Manville, in Smithfield. To hold property not exceeding in value ten thousand dollars.

1836. Reuben Mowry, Alexander Barney, Abner Ballou, Phillips Hill, John Jenckes, Jeremiah Smith, Willard Smith, Lewis Dexter, Daniel Jenckes, George L. Barnes, Samuel B. Harris, Thomas D. Holmes, Daniel C. Jenckes, G. H. Mowry, E. Ide, and those who should become members, were created a body corporate and politic, by the name of the Lime Rock Baptist Society, in Smithfield. The society was empowered to have and to hold real and personal estate not exceeding in all the sum of ten thousand dollars.

In 1837, the Representatives were instructed to use their exertions to procure the passage of an act authorizing the town to form itself into school districts; and that the said districts might tax themselves for the building of school houses, and might appoint each for itself a school committee. A petition was also by a unanimous vote addressed to the General Assembly as follows: "The Citizens of the Town of Smithfield, in Town Meeting assembled, would respectfully represent that they were incorporated in the year 1730 with all the *benefits* and *privileges* which other towns in this State have and enjoy; that at that time the population of the town was small; that they then sent two Representatives to the General Assembly, which, probably, was a fair representation for the then population. But since that time the population and business of the town has greatly increased; that in 1830 the population of the town was 6,853, and is believed now to be 8,000 or more; that in the early settlement of the town they were almost exclusively an agricultural people, but at the present time the pursuits of the citizens are extended to a greater variety of occupations than almost any other town in this State. The citizens of this town are free to admit that a larger town ought not to be entitled to the same representation in proportion to its population as a small one, but they do say, that such a gross inequality of representation as now exists in this State, ought to be corrected *without delay*. When the citizens of this town look at the present representation from the several towns in the State and see that the town of Portsmouth with a population of about 1,700, sends four Representatives to the State Legislature and this town but two they see that one freeman in Portsmouth has about the same representation in the legislature of the State as twenty freemen in Smithfield; to which the citizens of this town are unwilling longer silently to submit.

Wherefore they would respectfully request the General Assembly to take the subject of the extreme inequality of the present representation from the several towns in this State under consideration, and in such manner as seems most practicable and just correct the evil complained of."

1838. George Aldrich, 4th, George H. Mowry, William H. Gardner and others were incorporated by the name of the Lime Rock Library; to hold property not exceeding five thousand dollars.

At the June session, 1838, George O. Smith and others preferred a petition for the division of Smithfield, and at the January session, 1839, the petitioners, at their own request, had leave to withdraw their petition.

In the year 1839, the town council was instructed not to grant licenses for the sale of intoxicating liquors in less

amount than one gallon; and a committee was appointed to
examine into the expenses of the town as to the support of
the poor since the purchase of the town farm, and make a
detailed statement. In 1840, Arnold Spear, Lewis Dexter
and Dexter Aldrich were appointed a committee to draft
rules and regulations for the management of the town farm,
and the poor of the town. It was also provided that a committee of three be appointed to examine persons proposing
to teach in the schools; this committee was also to recommend school books, and visit the schools. The first school
committee, chosen in town meeting, consisted of Amos D.
Lockwood, Nicholas S. Winsor and Samuel S. Mallery. The
school committee was enlarged so as to consist of five persons.
Spencer Mowry was appointed to consider the expediency
of building a stone arch bridge over the easterly stream at
Woonsocket Falls, and negotiate with the town of Cumberland; the expense to Smithfield to be not over four hundred
dollars. James I. Harkness was appointed on the school
committee in place of Mr. Lockwood, who declined to serve,
and Thomas D. Holmes and David W. Aldrich were added
to said committee. The town council was instructed not
to grant license to any person to exhibit Circus Sports or
performances. Twelve hundred and seventy-three $\frac{13}{100}$ dollars were voted to George Olney as the committee who had
built Whipple's bridge. In 1841, the sum of three thousand
dollars was appropriated for the repair of highways, and one
thousand dollars for the public schools. As early as 1828,
it had been voted that the money appropriated for the public schools should be divided; one-half equally among the
several districts, and the other half according to the number
of scholars from four to twenty years old; and in 1829 an
appropriation of five hundred dollars was made, which was
increased in 1830 to six hundred dollars, and in 1831 to one
thousand dollars; no school tax appears as of record to
have been levied in 1832, but in 1837 a tax of one thousand

dollars was levied for school purposes, and this sum was annually appropriated until the year 1843, when it was reduced to five hundred dollars, but was raised in 1844 to one thousand dollars.

October, 1841, Samuel Withington, Silas W. Plympton, George W. Steere, Edward H. Adams, Simeon Newton, Hiram Bennett, Daniel F. Knapp, David Daniels, Edward H. Sprague, Lyman Cook, Arnold Briggs, Ozias M. Morse, Thomas A. Paine, Seth Chapin, and such as should become members hereafter, were created a body corporate and politic, by the name of The Congregational Society of Woonsocket Village, in Smithfield. They were entitled to hold property of every description not exceeding the value of twenty thousand dollars.

At a town meeting held on the 31 day of August, 1841, Stephen Steere, John Jenckes, Charles Moies and George Aldrich were appointed delegates from this town to attend a Convention to be holden at Providence, on the first Monday of November next, to frame a new Constitution for this State, either in whole or in part, with full powers for that purpose.

A town meeting was held on the twenty-first, twenty-second and twenty-third days of March, 1842, to vote for the ratification or rejection of the Constitution adopted by the Constitutional Convention, held in Providence on the first Monday in November, 1841.

The vote of the town of Smithfield was:

For Ratification.... 334
For Rejection.......... 993

In August of this year, Samuel B. Harris, Charles Moies, Nathan B. Sprague and Edward H. Sprague were chosen delegates to attend a Convention to be holden at Newport, on the second Monday of September next, to frame a new Constitution for this State, either in whole or in part, with full power for that purpose.

At a town meeting held on the twenty-first, twenty-second and twenty-third days of November, 1842, held to vote for the adoption or rejection of the Constitution proposed by the Constitutional Convention held at Newport in September preceding; and also to vote upon the question, whether in case the said proposed Constitution be adopted, the blank in the first line of section second, of article second of said Constitution, shall be filled by the word "White." Upon counting the votes there appeared:

> For Adoption 374
> For Rejection .... None.
> For filling the blank with the word "White "... 54
> Against so filling the blank 302

May, 1842, the Wionkheige Library, upon the petition of Harris Wing, was revived, and Robert Harris authorized to call the first meeting.

June, 1843, the petition of Charles Moies and others, that the town of Smithfield may be divided, was continued.

1843. David Clark, Isaac Smith, Alfred Arnold, E. S. Barrows, Peleg B. Sherman, A. Palsey, Daniel W. Luther, and such other males as now compose the Lonsdale Baptist Church, and such others as may become members of this corporation, were incorporated by the name of the First Baptist Society in Lonsdale, Smithfield; for the purpose of establishing and maintaining the worship of Almighty God, according to the rites and ordinances of the Baptist denomination, as practiced by the Warren Association.

At the June town meeting in 1844, the town council was requested to obtain annually, hereafter from the town treasurer, and other officers having the disbursement of the public money, a statement of the items, under general heads of the expenditures by them made; and this information was to be made public. In 1845, the school committee was reduced to three, and the members were to be paid one dollar

per day each, when engaged in their duties as such committee. This year the town voted 573 to 86 against the granting of licenses. Two thousand dollars was appropriated in
1846 for the public schools, and the committee allowed inci-
dental expenses in addition to one dollar per day. The
town council was authorized to audit, settle and order paid
all accounts and demands against the town of less amount
than fifty dollars. Thomas Buffum was appointed a committee to negotiate with the town of Cumberland in relation
to the widening the westerly arch bridge at Woonsocket.
The Senator and Representatives were instructed, in November, as it seems at a meeting specially called therefor, to oppose any dismemberment of the town. It was also voted
unanimously not to divide the town. At the June town
meeting, 1847, the town treasurer was requested to make
thereafter, to the annual town meeting in June, a statement
in writing of the situation of the town treasury. Five hundred copies of the report of the school committee were
ordered published. Three hundred dollars was appropriated
in 1848, to purchase safes for the safe keeping of the town
records. In 1849, the town voted 417 to 355 in favor of
granting licenses. This year the town voted to raise the
highway tax in money. The appropriations for bridges and
highways begin to increase notably.

1845. Joseph Wood, Hiram Wilmarth, John Moies, Samuel Wood, Sylvester C. Pierce, Pardon White, and their
associates, were incorporated by the name of the Central
Falls Congregational Society; for the purpose of erecting
and maintaining a meeting house for the public worship of
Almighty God, in the village of Central Falls, Smithfield,
R. I., and for the purpose of supporting and promulgating
the Christian religion, according to the rites and usages
of the Trinitarian Congregational Churches in the United
States.

At the January session of the General Assembly, 1845, Smithfield was divided into four districts, for voting purposes.

District No. 1 comprised all that portion of the town lying northerly of a line drawn from the Blackstone river at the Mott Dam, so called, to the junction of the Branch, and Providence and Douglass turnpikes, near the residence of Ethan Harris; and from said junction, following the said Providence and Douglass turnpikes, northeasterly to the line of Burrillville.

District No. 2 was bounded as follows: Beginning at the said junction of the Branch, and Providence and Douglass turnpikes, near the residence of Ethan Harris; thence northeasterly, following said Providence and Douglass turnpikes to the road leading to Martin's way, at the corner near Daniel Angell's tavern house; thence easterly with said road to the four corners, so called; thence southerly, following the road to the Louisquissett turnpike, near the brick school house, and following the said road easterly to the old Providence and Worcester road to a drift-way near the Smith lime-kiln; thence easterly, following said drift-way to the river road, so called; thence crossing said river road, near the Joseph Wilkinson house, and following a straight line and the nearest course to the Blackstone river.

District No. 3, bounded northerly by said District No. 2, easterly by the town of Cumberland, southerly by the town of North Providence, and westerly by the Providence and Douglass turnpike.

District No. 4, comprised that part of the town which lay southerly and southwesterly of the Providence and Douglass turnpike.

October, 1846, James Barber, George C. Ballou, Edward H. Sprague, George S. Wardwell, Amos D. Lockwood, William S. Slater, their associates and successors, were created a body corporate and politic, for the purpose of erecting
10

and supporting a Seminary of Learning in the town of Smithfield, in the vicinity of Woonsocket, by the name of the Smithfield Union Institute.

The June town meeting of 1850 was a laborious one. An unusual number of propositions were made to instruct the town council to lay out highways, and for appropriations for bridges; most of them were indefinitely postponed. The appropriation for the public schools, which had been for the three preceding years twenty-five hundred dollars, was raised to three thousand dollars; the school committee was increased to four members; the town council was requested to put up the collection of the town tax to the lowest bidder; the town treasurer, with the town clerk, were required to make a printed report showing the items for all moneys received and paid out for the town, and eight hundred copies of said report were to be printed for distribution. The town clerk was requested to prepare a tax book, and have five hundred copies thereof printed.

In 1851, three thousand dollars was appropriated for the public schools, and four thousand dollars for repairs of highways, to be paid in labor or money at the option of the persons and corporations taxed. This shows that the town was not ready to pay for, or do its highway work in the most efficient manner. Asa Winsor, Spencer Mowry and Thomas Steere were appointed a committee to revise the act of the town for repairing highways, passed August, 1819. It was voted, and the vote is a significant one, that: "Whenever the tax payers in any part of the town wish to apply in town meeting for an appropriation for the building a new road or bridge, the same shall be inserted in the town meeting warrant calling said meeting." The sum of five hundred dollars was appropriated for the purchase of safes to keep the most important records; the former appropriation of three hundred dollars having, doubtless, proved insufficient, and no action taken by virtue of it.

1851. James H. Eames, Nathan B. Sprague, Sessions Mowry, Anthony Steere, A. W. Ballou, Darius Hawkins, James Ainsworth, James Sikes, William Tinkham, J. S. Steere and others were incorporated by the name of St. Thomas Church, Greenville, in the town of Smithfield, Rhode Island; for the purpose of establishing and maintaining public worship, according to the rites and usages of the Protestant Episcopal Church in the United States of America. The corporation was empowered to hold property not exceeding twenty-five thousand dollars.

In 1852, four thousand five hundred dollars were appropriated for the public schools; four thousand for highways. The several reports were taken up and disposed of. The bill reported by the committee to revise the highway law was enacted a law, and one thousand copies ordered printed.

In 1853, the town treasurer was directed to be still more particular in the statements of the amount of taxes, and the amount collected; his report was to be audited by the auditors of accounts, and by them certified. Four thousand five hundred dollars was appropriated for the public schools. The school committee was to consist of only three persons, the town council being requested to appoint only so many; and no school teacher was to be a school committee-man.

At the several district meetings of the town, held on the 28th day of June, 1853, for the election of delegates to meet in Convention at the State House, in Providence, on the ninth day of August, A. D. 1853, for the purpose of forming a Constitution of government for this State, the following delegates were elected: Gideon Bradford, Thomas Steere, Welcome B. Sayles, Robert Harris, Daniel Pearce, James O. Whitney and Asa Winsor.

1853. Harvey Chace, Samuel B. Chace and Oliver Chace incorporated by the name of the Valley Falls Company.

1853. Zachariah Allen, Philip Allen, Richard Waterman

and Amos D. Smith made a body corporate by the name and style of the Stillwater Reservoir Company.

1854.   Dexter Lime Rock Company incorporated.

In 1854, the appropriations for schools and the repairs of highways were each four thousand five hundred dollars. Greater strictness was imposed upon the town treasurer in preparing his accounts, and he was allowed from that year, and for that year, the salary of fifty dollars.   Charles Moies, Amasa Smith and Smith R. Mowry were appointed a committee to report the best system of repairing highways and bridges.   The town meeting recommended to the town council to reappoint the then three school committee men. A building was ordered to be erected for the accommodation of the insane poor of the town, which poor were supported by the town at the Butler Insane Asylum, in Providence.   Spencer Mowry was appointed the committee, and the building was to be built at a cost not exceeding one thousand dollars.

In 1855, L. C. Tourtellot, Samuel Clarke, Samuel Clarke, Jr., Jacob Arnold and Jacob Bicknell, and their associates, were constituted a body politic and corporate by the name of the Moriah Library Association.

At the June meeting in 1855, the report of the committee on repairing highways was laid on the table.   The schools and highways received each an appropriation of forty-five hundred dollars.   The school committee was required to have its accounts for services audited and presented to the annual June town meeting for settlement.   The building of the insane hospital by Spencer Mowry was reported.   Two thousand dollars was appropriated to construct a stone arch bridge across the Branch river at Slatersville; William S. Slater made verbal proposals to build said bridge, and the details were such as to show that a most substantial structure was contemplated.   In the Warrant had been included this

question: "That the town of Smithfield be divided; beginning at the dividing line between the towns of Burrillville and Glocester, thence running Easterly parallel with
the South line of said town of Smithfield, to the Blackstone
river." The vote was as follows:

In the affirmative..................... 63
In the negative..........:.... 61
                                                    ———
                                                    124

Upon the question: "To appoint a committee for the
purpose of opposing the petition now pending before the
General Assembly, praying to set off a portion of the town
of Smithfield and of Cumberland into a town to be called
Woonsocket;" it was voted that Robert Harris be a committee to oppose said petition.

1856. Obed Paine, Elisha Steere, Winsor Farnum, William Steere, Robert Harris, Ezra Whitford, Jabez W. Mowry,
James Armington, William G. Perry, William Patt and
others were incorporated by the name of the Georgiaville
Evangelical Society, having for its object the building of a
house of public worship in Georgiaville, in the town of
Smithfield, and the more effectually promoting the diffusion
of the benevolent principles of Christianity in the village
and town aforesaid.

The business at the June town meeting, 1856, was of a
routine character. The appropriations for public schools
are now so much a matter of course that they will not be
noticed when of the ordinary character. They have been
put on the same footing as the highways, and are as regularly and fully provided for.

In June, 1858, "An act regulating the financial affairs of
the town of Smithfield," was presented by Charles Moies,
"and after a debate of great length," it was rejected by a
vote of 57 to 37. Whereupon it was referred to Joseph

Almy, Daniel Hale and William H. Seagraves, as a committee to frame amendments thereto; which committee reported it back to the meeting, with a recommendation that it pass. Upon vote it was rejected. The bills of physicians for attendance upon the poor of the town were ordered to be audited, by the auditors of accounts, and presented to the annual town meeting for allowance. The treasurer was directed to make estimates of the probable expenses for the ensuing year; he was also directed to secure a proper distribution of his report before the day of the annual meeting. And no money was to be paid out of the town treasury between the day of concluding his report and the day of the annual meeting.

1859. Oren A. Ballou, Stephen N. Mason and George S. Wardwell incorporated as the Hamlet Manufacturing Company.

At the annual town meeting, held on the 11th of June, 1861, it was voted: That the town council be and they are hereby empowered to appoint a committee, consisting of seven persons, whose duty it shall be to investigate and enquire into the condition of those families residing in said town of Smithfield, of which the members thereof have volunteered their services in the defence of the country during the unhappy troubles now existing throughout the land; that said committee shall be empowered whenever they deem it necessary that assistance should be rendered to such families, to draw on the town treasurer, with an order from the town council for such sum of money as is deemed by them requisite for the use and benefit of such families. It being understood, the assistance in the above cases rendered shall not be deemed, or so reported in the town treasurer's report as "expenses for support of poor;" but shall be kept separate, and reported as moneys paid to families of the volunteers in the internal war now existing. Voted, That said committee shall serve without pecuniary compensation.

On the 29th of June, the town council appointed Joseph Wood, Anthony Steere and Harvey S. Bartlett a committee for the distribution of the moneys appropriated for the benefit of the families of the volunteers; and on the 27th of July, the council ordered forty-two dollars and eighty-six cents to be paid Joseph Wood, as having been expended by him as one of said committee. On the 31st of August, Joseph Wood was allowed fifty-three dollars and seventy-four cents as said committee-man, for the relief to soldiers' families. September 13th, Arlon Mowry was appointed by the council, " Volunteer Relief Committee, for said town." On the 28th of September, one hundred and twenty dollars was appropriated for the benefit of soldiers' families; and William P. Steere was appointed relief committee. On the 27th of October, two hundred dollars was voted to the committee of relief. In November, two hundred and twenty-six$\frac{61}{100}$ dollars was voted said committee. In December, the relief committee was allowed four hundred and ninety-seven$\frac{44}{100}$ dollars; and George Kent was appointed relief committee for District No. 3, to assist soldiers' families; and Joseph W. Tillinghast was appointed assistant relief committee for said district.

At the January meeting of the town council, 1862, one hundred and eighty-one$\frac{43}{100}$ dollars were appropriated for the benefit of soldiers' families; and in February, the sum applied to, and for the same purpose, was four hundred and thirty-five$\frac{46}{100}$ dollars. For March, the amount so applied was five hundred and twenty-seven$\frac{15}{100}$ dollars. For April, the sum as aforesaid was four hundred and seventy-five dollars. For May, it amounted to three hundred and seventy-five dollars.

At the June town meeting, 1862, it was voted : That the town council be and they are hereby empowered to appoint a committee, consisting of not more than twelve persons, whose duty it shall be to enquire into the condition of those families residing in said town of Smithfield of which any members thereof are volunteers in the service of the United States. Said committee shall be empowered whenever in their opinion said families need assistance to help said families in such way as to said committee seems proper, and to present at the end of each and every month, to the town council of said town, a bill of such assistance rendered, and if acceptable by said town council, and allowed, said committee shall be paid out of the moneys in the hands of the town treasurer the amount of their said bill; which sums of money paid out by the town treasurer, shall be accounted for as relief to soldiers' families. Said committee to serve without compensation.

On the 30th of July, 1862, a special town meeting was held, and it was voted: That a committee of eight persons be appointed to draw resolutions in order to carry out the object of the meeting. William S. Slater, Stephen N. Mason, Lewis Dexter, Benoni Cooke, Charles Moies, Bailey E. Borden, William P. Steere and Jabez W. Mowry were chosen said committee.

The committee made the following report:

Whereas the President of the United States having issued his call for three hundred thousand men, in addition to those now in the military service of our country; and whereas it is desirable that this town be as prompt in the future, as in times past, in doing her duty in putting down the present rebellion; It is, therefore, Voted and ordered, that the sum of two hundred dollars be offered as a bounty, and to be paid to each and every able-bodied man, the whole number not to exceed one-hundred and thirty-eight, the quota of this town, as made out by the Adjutant General, who shall enlist by authority of the Governor of this State, for service under the call of the President of the United States, as originally issued, or as it may have been, or may hereafter be modified by the authority issuing it; to be paid to said volunteer so enlisting, in the following manner, to wit: Twenty-five dollars when he shall have passed a surgical examination and been sworn as provided by law; twenty-five dollars when mustered into the service of the United States, and the balance to be subject to his written order, in monthly installments of fifty dollars each, until the whole is paid.

The town treasurer was authorized to borrow the sum of twenty-seven thousand six hundred dollars to pay the bounties aforesaid. Stephen N. Mason, Samuel Clark, Bailey E. Borden and William Winsor were appointed a committee to draw orders for the payment of said bounties; said committee was given "discretionary powers" to advance and promote enlistments, and the sum of four hundred dollars was appropriated for its expenses.

At a special town meeting, held in September, it was voted that the committee appointed by the town council to assist the families of volunteers, should be paid such compensation for their services as the town council shall deem sufficient. Thomas Moies and James N. Woodward, for District No. 3, William T. Smith and Fenner Colwell, for District No. 1, and William A. Bishop and Benjamin A. Winsor, for District No. 4, were appointed recruiting officers for the town.

Voted: That the sum of one dollar per week be paid to the wife of each volunteer who may enlist in a company formed within the town of Smithfield; or if no wife, to his mother, if dependent, and fifty cents per week to each and every child, not including boys over sixteen years of age, and not to exceed the sum of twelve dollars per month to any one family.

The town council failed to appoint the committee of twelve, as empowered by the town, to disburse the money for the relief of soldiers' families, but continued through the year on the plan first adopted.

The disbursements were:

July	$796.03
August	513.37
September	419.25
October	459.69
November	693.51
December	773.91

11

1862.   Ezra Whitford, Richard Mowry, Daniel G. Aldrich, Smith Mowry, 2d, and such others as are or may become members of the corporation, were created a body corporate by the name of the Smithfield United Society, for the purpose of establishing and maintaining the worship of Almighty God.

May, 1863, Harvey Chace, Samuel B. Chace and Oliver Chace, were incorporated as the Manville Company.

1863.   Valuation of Smithfield, $6,806,850.

At the January session of the General Assembly, 1864, William Pooke, Simeon S. Steere, Nehemiah Tinkham, William Winsor, Daniel Champlin, William Tyler, William A. Steere, George P. Grant, James Grop, Stephen Steere, Daniel Winsor, Gideon Peckham, Philip L. Medbury, Harris Farnum, Allen Place and Henry Winsor, were incorporated by the name of the First Freewill Baptist Church of Smithfield, for religious purposes.

In June, 1864, the town gave the Council further authority in the matter of relief to the families of soldiers.   The war expenses of the town were nearly forty thousand dollars.

In 1866, six thousand dollars was appropriated for the public schools.

In 1867 eight thousand dollars was so appropriated.

1868.   Fourteen thousand dollars was so appropriated. Fifteen hundred dollars was appropriated towards building the " Dr. Ballou " bridge, so called, across the Blackstone river at Woonsocket.   Six thousand dollars was appropriated toward building a bridge at Central Falls.   Fifteen hundred dollars was appropriated toward building a bridge at the Albion.

In 1869, eighteen thousand dollars was appropriated for the use of the public schools.

Fifteen thousand dollars was appropriated for the repair of highways.

For building a pier for the Dr. Ballou bridge there was appropriated................................$ 250.00
To complete the bridge at Central Falls......... 2000.00
For bridges leading to the "Old Maids' Farm"... 500.00
For a culvert on Logee Hill................... 500.00
To grade Broad street, Central Falls........... 1500.00
For lamp posts, and lamps, and lights.......... 2500.00
For curbing................................. 2000.00

It was directed that the school committee should consist of six persons.

George Kilburn, Charles Moies, Nathaniel W. Spaulding and George W. Holt, who were appointed a committee, in 1868, to oppose the petition to have a part of the town of Smithfield set off to Woonsocket, were continued such committee.

The assessors of taxes were directed to view the estates of the town before fixing the valuation, when necessary, and they were allowed three dollars per day.

At the June town meeting, 1870, it was voted, that: A committee consisting of five persons be appointed to confer with the committee from the town of Woonsocket in the matter of setting off and annexing to said town of Woonsocket a portion of the town of Smithfield; said committee to report to an adjourned meeting.

Voted, that said committee be appointed by nomination and vote.

Voted, that said committee be selected, two from district No. 1, and one from each of the other three districts of the town.

Voted, that Bradbury C. Hill, Stephen N. Mason, George Kilburn, Pardon Angell and Samuel Clark be, and they are hereby appointed a committee for the town of Smithfield, to confer with a committee from the town of Woonsocket, to see if any arrangement can be made satisfactory to both towns, whereby a portion of the town of Smithfield shall be set off and annexed to the town of Woonsocket. The committee was to report to an adjourned meeting.

Eighteen thousand dollars was appropriated for the use of the public schools, and one thousand dollars for evening schools.

At the adjourned meeting, aforementioned, Stephen N. Mason offered the following resolution :

Resolved : That the freemen of the town of Smithfield, in town meeting assembled, are favorable to a division of the town, setting off and annexing to the town of Woonsocket that part of the town which has been canvassed by the committee.

Upon vote taken, the result was declared by the moderator to be :

In favor thereof..................... 42
Opposed........................... 193

Thomas Steere, George A. Kent, Bradbury C. Hill, John A. Adams and Pardon Angell were appointed a committee to investigate concerning an article published in the Providence Journal against the overseer of the poor, the keeper of the town asylum, and the commissioners of the town asylum, and the general treatment of the poor. Said committee to have power to send for persons and papers, to report to the town council, and to publish their proceedings in pamphlet form for distribution, and the result of the investigation to be published in the Providence Journal.

The report of this committee was made to the town council in December, and copies thereof were directed by the council to be distributed among the taxpayers of the town.

At a special town meeting, held on the 21st of January, 1871, to take into consideration the subject of dividing the town of Smithfield into three towns, and establishing the boundary lines thereof, the following question was put:
Shall the town of Smithfield be divided or not?
The vote was:

In the affirmative.....................111
In the negative...................... 33
                                   ———
                                    144

It was then voted that this meeting favors a division of the town of Smithfield, according to the act now on the Moderator's table.

This bill, which was carefully considered, was the bill which was passed by the General Assembly, with a few unimportant alterations.

On the 25th of March, 1871, the town council appointed Thomas Steere, Thomas Barnes and Joseph W. Tillinghast a committee to investigate the matter of the claims for damages by the abutting proprietors on Washington street, Central Falls.

Charles Moies, Thomas Steere and Thomas Barnes were appointed a committee to examine claims made for damages by reason of the grading of Broad street.

The direct action which resulted in the division of the town of Smithfield originated in a petition to the General Assembly, at its January session, 1867. This petition was continued to the May, and again to the January session, 1868. At the May session, 1868, the House Judiciary Committee recommended the continuance of the petition, submitting as the opinion of the committee that some action should be taken (by the town) tending to remedy the grievances complained of growing out of the present organization of the town of Smithfield. At the January session,

1869, the majority—four out of five—of the Joint Special Committee, to whom this matter of the division of the town had been referred, made a very elaborate report, recommending such division. A minority report was also made. The "Act" reported by the committee was laid on the table. Another petition, being substantially a continuation of the proceedings commenced in 1867, was preferred to the January session of the General Assembly, 1870. It was continued to the May session and then to the January session, 1871. After repeated hearings, the Joint Special Committee, upon the open or tacit agreement of the parties concerned, recommended the passage of the bill which had been drawn, and the town was, by the General Assembly, divided.

CHAPTER III.

MANUFACTURING AND MECHANICAL INDUSTRY.

NO proper idea of the value of Smithfield, or of Rhode Island, as the home of inventive genius and persevering industry can be had without a slight acquaintance, at least, with the skill and work of the early Wilkinsons.

Israel Wilkinson was born in Smithfield, in 1711, near Manville, at which place he built the "Unity Furnace," so long a prominent landmark in the town. He also built, in conjunction with Nicholas and Moses Brown, of Providence, and others, the "Hope Furnace," in Cranston. He was called to Boston to aid in casting cannon previous to the Revolution. On one occasion, the workmen in Boston having found it impossible to extract the "core," Mr. Wilkinson was sent for, and upon his departure, his wife, with a womanly and Quaker-like prudence, said to him: "Israel, see to it that they pay thee well." Upon his return, entertaining no doubt of his mechanical success, but doubtful as to the pecuniary reward, she asked him what he had been given. To which the good Friend made answer: "As good a bowl of punch as ever a man drank."

Oziel Wilkinson was born in Smithfield, and was a mechanic from a boy. His father had a blacksmith shop on Mussey's brook, a small stream which empties into the Blackstone river, just above Albion. He was afterwards associated with Samuel Slater in manufacturing cotton yarn at Pawtucket. Said Slater married one of his daughters.

David Wilkinson, son of Oziel, worked with his father in the shop, and was the inventor of the sliding lathe, in 1794, for which he received a patent in 1798, although from it he received no pecuniary advantage. In 1848, Congress made an appropriation of ten thousand dollars to him, "as a remuneration to him for the benefit accruing to the public service for the use of the principle of the guage and sliding lathe, of which he was the inventor, now in use in the workshops of the government at the different national armories and arsenals." He also invented and constructed a working engine, which was placed in one of John Brown's India ship's boats, operating successfully.

But it is the cotton manufacture which has been the prominent one in Smithfield, as in the State. And although Samuel Slater began his important work in Pawtucket, he soon came to Smithfield, and here his name is perpetuated in that of one of the most delightful of New England villages. His name is linked to the history of Smithfield, also, by his marriage with the daughter of one of the first and most enterprising mechanics of this town, which, in those early days, was famous for its shrewd, and capable and ingenious artisans.

To Samuel Slater belongs the honor of having introduced into this country, the manufacture, which, in its far extending influence, is greatly the most valuable in the land, and which affects in one way or another every inhabitant of the country. After food, clothing is the first necessity of life; and of all the materials provided by nature, cotton is the most extensively used, the world over. Samuel Slater witnessed the first crude experiments which were made in the endeavor to spin cotton by machinery. His name is associated, and honorably associated with those of Strutt and Arkwright. From the earliest ages cotton cloth has been manufactured in the East, where the plant is indigenous, but the yarn was, and is, spun upon the distaff, and the loom em-

ployed is simply a few sticks or reeds which the weaver
carries in his hands, and puts it up in the shade of a tree,
or at the side of his cottage, and moves from place to place,
as fancy dictates or the heat compels. An overspreading
branch, to which to fasten his balances, a hole in the ground
to hold his legs and the lower part of the "geer," and his
well trained muscles, supply the Indian with "privilege"
and "power." With this rude material, the East Indian
has for centuries produced fabrics, some of them so fine as
to be properly designated in the poetic language of the
Orient, "webs of woven wind," of such exquisite texture as
scarcely to be discerned under a heavy dew. But what
the manufacture was thousands of years ago, that it is to-
day. When the inhabitants of the British Isles were clothed
in skins, ere Cæsar had carried civilization and the sword
thither, the Indian artisan produced a fabric which is yet
equally a beauty and a wonder. But what he did then he
does now, and nothing more. This superior product was
the result of generations of training culminating with a few
individuals in extraordinary skill. The great bulk of the
cloth was of such quality as could easily be made by a great
majority of the inhabitants, and such as the every-day wants
of the population demanded. In the East there have been
no improvements, no inventions, no building up of towns
and opening up of new lands; the warp is still stretched on
the ground, and the operative is still half naked and wholly
ignorant. The introduction of machinery into India has
not proved successful. It has brought no profit to the
English, and subjugated the laborer to slavery.

In the year 1769, Richard Arkwright (afterwards Sir
Richard), obtained his patent for spinning with rollers,
and associated with him in business a Mr. Need, and Mr.
Strutt, the latter a man of great mechanical knowledge and
the largest business capacity. This firm erected the same
year a mill in Nottingham, worked by horse power, which

12

was superseded in 1771, by one built in Cromford, to which motion was given by water. In 1783, Samuel Slater entered the establishment of Strutt and Arkwright, and continued in their service for some eight years, having in the meantime not only become perfectly familiar with the whole routine of the business, but entirely capable, as it afterwards appeared, of constructing from memory the machinery re-quisite to spin the yarn. On the 15th day of September, 1789, Mr. Slater sailed from London for New York, where, after a passage of sixty-six days, he arrived, and whence he departed January, 1790, for Providence. On the 18th day of the same month, Moses Brown carried him to Pawtucket, and on the 20th day of December next following, he started three cards, drawing and roving, and seventy-two spindles, which were worked by an old fulling mill water wheel in a clothiers building, in which the business of Almy, Brown & Slater was continued for about twenty months, at the expiration of which time they had several thousand pounds of yarn on hand, notwithstanding every exertion was used to weave and sell it.

It is almost impossible to conceive the difficulties which surrounded and impeded the success of Slater. He was a stranger in a strange land; there was no person who had ever worked upon such machinery as he proposed to construct; there were no machine shops; few skilled workmen either in wood or iron, and no facilities for him in the accomplishment of his designs; he had not even the roughest sketch of his machines; he had only a tenacious memory, a thorough knowledge of what was wanted, and an indomitable will. Fortunately he found at once in Oziel Wilkinson, one, who like himself possessed a keen mind and a mechanical genius. They together made, or superintended the making, of the necessary tools to be used, and amid all the discouragements, and they were neither few nor small, which Mr. Slater encountered, he ever found in

Mr. Wilkinson a friend and an adviser. Up to this time, no carding or spinning machinery had been successfully operated, and none at all by water. Tristam Burges, in Congress, paid this eloquent tribute to these men, to whom Rhode Island owes so much: "A circumstance worthy the attention of the whole nation, and worthy, also, of a fair page in her history, is the art and mystery of making cloth with machinery moved by water power. This was introduced into Rhode Island, and commenced in Pawtucket, four miles from Providence, about the same time that the American system was established, by the import law of July 4th, 1789. Samuel Slater, an English mechanic of the first order of mental ability, brought this invention to Pawtucket. He could not bring out from England, models, draughts or specifications, the whole art was treasured in his own mind; that alone, which could not be rummaged and pillaged by any custom house regulation. He, on his arrival, addressed himself to Oziel Wilkinson & Sons. They were blacksmiths, whose hands were as skillful as their minds were intelligent and persevering. I have often thought Divine Providence directed Slater, and brought him to lay his projects before the Wilkinsons; because He had not fitted any other men in this country, with minds and abilities, either to see, and at once comprehend the immense benefit of it, or to understand and perform what must be understood and performed to bring this scheme into full and perfect operation." In a word, when Samuel Slater arrived in this country, all the machinery in use for the manufacture of cotton yarn for warps, was so imperfect as to preclude success, and there was a desire to import yarn from India, the American people being wholly indebted to and dependent upon Great Britain for cotton goods.

And here we must be permitted to interrupt our narrative by the relation of an anecdote which as completely discloses the character of Samuel Slater as it indubitably proves him to have been a man of the highest moral tone. After his frames were ready for operation, he prepared the cotton and started his cards; the cotton rolled on the top cards, instead of passing through the small cylinder. This was a great perplexity to him, and he was for several days in great agitation. Mrs. Oziel Wilkinson, in whose house he boarded, perceiving his distress, said to him: "Art thou sick, Samuel?" To which he replied by explaining the obstacle he had met, and saying: "If I am frustrated in my carding machine, they will think me an impostor." It was not of his fame, but of his honor, he was thinking.

It is perhaps as well to observe just here that up to the year 1817 the operations of manufactories in this country were confined, save in one mill in Massachusetts, to spinning yarn only, which was put out in webs and wove by hand-loom weavers. Mules for spinning filling had not then been introduced. From 1791 to 1805 all, or nearly all, the cotton factories erected in this country were built under the direction of men who had acquired their knowledge of the necessary machinery while in Mr. Slater's employ. In 1799 Mr. Slater entered into company with Oziel Wilkinson, Timothy Greene and William Wilkinson, the two latter, as well as himself, having married daughters of Oziel Wilkinson. They built the second mill on the east side of the Pawtucket river, the firm being Samuel Slater and Company, Mr. Slater holding one half of the stock. The year 1829 was a disastrous one to the manufacturers of Rhode Island. Mr. Slater felt but withstood the shock. His own business was perfectly within control. It had always been managed with great prudence, and his estate was, for those days, a very large one. Owing to endorsements he had made for friends, and which he had to meet, he suffered a temporary embarrassment, but paid his own paper and his endorsements, and retained a property gained by honest industry and careful attention, and which was thereafter

largely increased. Mr. Slater died at Webster, Massachusetts, April 20th, 1835, aged 67.

It will be seen at once that the success of Samuel Slater
was the result of a profound knowledge of his business; an
unalterable determination; constant labor; and the most
scrupulous integrity. From the commencement of his career
to its close, his whole course was distinguished by diligence,
sagacity and uprightness. His letters to his business cor-
respondents display shrewdness, breadth of view and a
straight forward manliness; those to his children, a very
affectionate though not particularly demonstrative disposition. Fortunate in his early opportunities, they were yet
such as would neither have been appreciated nor improved
by one less observing, less faithful or less persevering. Respected in life, his character loses nothing, to say the least,
in comparison with the more modern ideas of the market
place and the counting room. In a word; in his exactness
of purpose; his thoroughness in oversight; his unwearied
exertion, and his perfect and unswerving regard for the
fulfilment of every obligation he assumed, he may well be
cited as a man whose example it would be both safe and
honorable to follow. Those who attain any excellence, said
Dr. Johnson, uttering a truth founded upon the experience
of mankind, commonly spend life in one common pursuit,
for excellence is not often gained upon easier terms. He
who spent a life in the pursuit of excellence, in that which
of itself was most excellent, and spent it honestly and honorably, may well, by his influence, say:

> " Let none presume
> To wear an undeserved dignity.
> O, that estates, degrees and offices,
> Were not derived corruptly! and that clear honor
> Were purchased by the merit of the wearer!
> How many then should cover, that stand bare!
> How many be commanded, that command!
> How much low peasantry would then be gleaned
> From the true seed of honor! and how much honor
> Pick'd from the chaff and ruin of the times,
> To be new varnish'd!"

In May, 1806, the village of Slatersville was begun. The natural location was beautiful in the extreme. The mills are situated in an amphitheatre, with the river on one side, and some acres of meadow on the other. On a plateau is the village, consisting of well built houses, many of them large and elegant. In the centre of the village is a common, well planted with trees, and fronting it the Congregational Church, a commodious and well proportioned building. The fall of water is 37 feet. 1,407,414 pounds of cotton are manufactured annually, by means of 26,824 spindles and 605 looms. Six hundred hands are employed, and the annual product is 5,799,541 yards of sheeting, shirting, flannel and print goods. The population is 1,200. The value of the yearly product is $600,000. The First National Bank, of Smithfield, is located here, with a capital of one hundred thousand dollars. The village library possesses one thousand volumes; no liquor is allowed to be sold in the place, and neatness and good order prevail. "If," said Tristam Burges, in Congress, "if manufacturing establishments are a benefit and a blessing to the Union, the name of Slater must ever be held in grateful remembrance by the American people."

FORESTDALE.

This thriving village is situated on the Branch river, about one mile below Slatersville. The first business engaged in here, of any importance, was that of the manufacture of scythes, by Newton Darling, about the year 1824. Mr. Darling had learned his trade of Col. Comstock Passmore, at Branch village. The water power cost Mr. Darling only one hundred dollars and the cost of sluice way, to be opened only when water ran over the dam. H. S. Mansfield afterwards joined Mr. Darling in the business. In 1839, Ansel Holman joined the firm. In 1841, Mr. Darling sold out his interest and the firm became Mansfield & Holman. It was afterwards

Mansfield & Lamb, Estus Lamb having become a partner, and the firm owning the entire village. Prior to 1860 the annual product was 10,000 dozen of scythes; since, it has been about 8,000 dozen. During the war of the rebellion this firm furnished the government with thirty thousand sabres, officially declared to be equal to any manufactured in the country. In 1860, the firm erected a stone cotton mill, which is operated by the Forestdale Manufacturing Company. The mill is 166x68 feet, three stories high; with an ell 65x45 feet, of the same height. The fall is 14 feet. Horse power—water, 250; steam, 80. In the scythe works 150 tons of iron are annually used; 3 tons of steel, and 100 grindstones are employed. The Forestdale Company use annually 1,400 bales of cotton, run 15,000 spindles, and 300 looms, employing 250 hands. The gross product is 2,000,-000 yards of cloth, valued at (1870) $300,000. The tenement houses, sixty-one in number, for both establishments, are two stories in height; there are two excellent boarding houses, and the whole place is neat, orderly and attractive.

BRANCH VILLAGE.

This once considerable, but now unimportant place, is situated on the Branch river, about one mile north of Union Village. In the year 1795, Elisha Bartlett came here from Glocester, and commenced the manufacture of scythes, which business he continued till his death, in 1804. Afterwards Col. Comstock Passmore purchased the place. A small cotton mill was erected here by William Buffum and sons, Otis Bartlett, Comstock Passmore, and perhaps some others. It is now standing. The mill was operated by Col. Passmore, who died about the year 1825. Otis Bartlett carried on the scythe making business thereafter. The mill has been run for the manufacture of cloth or warps, at different times, and by various parties until nearly the present time; David Daniels, David M. Daniels, Alfred Morse, Joseph Morse, and

Emor Coe, having occupied it, but none of them with any permanent profit. The privilege is a good one, but the mill is very small, and it has followed the path of small mills. The privilege and land are now owned by the Blackstone Manufacturing Company.

WATERFORD.

Evans and Seagrave, and Earl P. Mason, operate one of the woolen mills at Waterford, formerly owned by Welcome Farnum. The fall of water is 10 feet; horse power—steam, 160; water, 300. Hands employed, 400; looms, 58 broad, 52 narrow; setts of machinery, 24; pounds of wool used annually, 1,000,000; tons of coal, 1,000; gallons of oil, 1,000. The product is 700,000 yards of fancy cassimeres.

F. M. BALLOU

also runs one of the Waterford mills, with 10 feet fall; 100 horse power, water; 160 hands; 50 narrow looms; 10 setts of machinery, and producing yearly 300,000 yards of fancy cassimeres.

CHARLES B. ALDRICH,

contractor and builder, is located at Waterford. He uses 40 horse power, steam; employs 50 hands.

THE WOONSOCKET GAS COMPANY

consumes 2,300 tons of coal, and makes annually 11,131,000 feet of gas.

THE ENTERPRISE COMPANY.

This company was organized in 1870, and built a mill upon the estate known as "The Old Maid's Farm," between Woonsocket and Waterford. The business is that of making lastings, serges, &c., and produces, annually, 375,000 yards. The officers are:

President—John D. Nichols.

Treasurer—Ruel P. Smith.

Superintendent—S. N. Lougee.

GLOBE MILLS, WOONSOCKET.

In 1827, Thomas Arnold, Marble Shove and Thomas A. Paine purchased five or six acres of land, and one-fourth part of the flow of the Blackstone river, for which they paid ten thousand dollars. Two small brooks added something to the water power. There was a saw mill on the premises, but no other improvements. They built a cotton mill, a corn mill, "Globe" store, two dwelling houses and a barn. The cotton mill was 36x72 feet, three stories high and attic. Fall, 16½ feet. Two thousand spindles, fifty looms. They made cloth and warps. In winter of 1829–30, they sold to Samuel Shove, by assignee. He built one dwelling house and machine shop. His assignee sold, in 1834, to Thomas Sprague & Sons, who held until about the year 1837, when Vaughan and E. H. Sprague came into possession. From them it passed into the hands of George C. Ballou, who also owns and runs a steam saw mill four stories high, in which is also machinery for planing, mortising and sash making, He has also laid the foundation for a new cotton mill to be 70x234 feet, with an ell 50x147 feet.

THE WOONSOCKET COMPANY,

Owning four fine mills, and originally what is now the village of Bernon, much of which it still retains, occupies a large and valuable privilege, and has done much for that village. In 1831, the late Samuel Greene came from Pawtucket to this place, and up to within a few months of his decease had charge of the company's establishment.

13

He was born in 1791, and his mother was daughter of Oziel Wilkinson. He possessed a decided taste for mechanics, and was, perhaps, more scientifically informed in the science of hydraulics than any other of our manufacturers. When Gilmore first came to Rhode Island for the purpose of constructing the power loom, Mr. Greene made his acquaintance, and obtained from him much valuable information. In 1820, he, with others, formed a company under the name of the "Pawtucket Worsted Company." To the late Hon. N. R. Knight, when he was chosen Senator of the United States from this State, the company presented a vest of their own manufacture, which he wore to Washington, and which attracted considerable attention as being the first specimen of worsted goods manufactured in the United States.

Mr. Greene represented his native town in the General Assembly from 1816 to 1821, inclusive. He was a consistent member of the Episcopal Church, and "St. James' Church," in Bernon, was aided by his counsels and his contributions. The grounds of the Woonsocket Company's mills are large, beautifully kept and adorned with magnificent trees.

The company employ in these mills 250 hands, run 288 looms and 13,000 spindles.

HAMLET.

Situated half a mile below Woonsocket, is one of the prettiest villages on the Blackstone river. Its first proprietors were Edward H. Carrington and Stephen H. Smith.

Edward H. Carrington was one of the best known and most highly accomplished merchants of Providence in his day.

Stephen H. Smith was a scion of good Rhode Island stock, being a descendant of John Smith, the miller, of the early Providence records.

In 1830, the land about the Hamlet was covered with a

dense growth of wood; there was no road leading to Woonsocket. The mill originally contained only 7,000 spindles. It was erected by Spencer Mowry, Esq. The best carpenters were paid $20 per month and boarded. The mill passed into the hands of Edward Carrington, Jr., and George S. Wardwell. It is now owned by Isaac M. Bull, who has greatly enlarged it, and filled it with improved machinery. The main part is 212 feet long, by 40 in width, with an addition 50x40 feet, and the foundation is laid for another addition of the same size. It is run by three turbine wheels. The fall is 9.5 feet; power, 325. Hands employed, 200; looms, 300; spindles, 15,500. Pounds of cotton used annually, 676,000; number of yards of cloth manufactured, 2,700,000.

MANVILLE.

This pleasant village is situated four miles south of Woonsocket, on the Blackstone river, and the Manville Company own, but do not occupy, the entire volume of the water. A history of this place will show very intelligibly the history of manufacturing operations in this State, after the smaller streams were left for larger privileges, and even before the latter had become generally profitable. In 1740, the land on which the village is now built, on both sides of the river, was owned by David Wilkinson, who, in that year, deeded it to Samuel Wilkinson, who, in 1747, redeeded it to David. In 1759, David Wilkinson deeded it to Benjamin Wing of Dartmouth, Massachusetts. Wing conveyed it to Abner Bartlett, in 1802, in which deed the premises is for the first time referred to as a "water privilege," and mention is made of the bridge, by the name of the "Unity Bridge." In 1803, Bartlett sold to Luke Jillson, who conveyed it, in 1805, to Samuel Hill, Jr., of Smithfield, and William Aldrich, of Cumberland. Samuel Hill, Jr., was known afterwards as Judge Hill. Hill and Aldrich deeded, in 1811, to Thomas Man, Stephen Clark, George Hill, David Hill, Jesse Brown, George Aldrich, Otis Capron, David Wilkinson, Alpheus Ammidon, Stephen Whipple, and Asa Bartlett, reserving an interest to themselves, and the grantees were styled the "Unity Manufacturing Company." Three years thereafter, in 1814, Aaron Man, father of Samuel F. Man, purchased the interest of Alpheus Ammidon, and allusion is made in the conveyance to the Unity Cotton factory, a grist mill, saw mill, and fulling mill. In 1821, the Unity Manufacturing Company sold to William Jenkins and Samuel F. Man, all their interest in the estate. In 1831, Jenkins and Man conveyed one-fourth part of the estate to Arlon Man, brother of Samuel F., the estate having been considerably enlarged by purchases of adjoining land, since the original purchase from Wilkinson ; September 28, 1854, the heirs of Samuel F. Man, and William and Anna Jenkins, conveyed the mill estate and lands to the Valley Falls Company. In 1863, the Valley Falls Company deeded to the Manville Company, then composed of Tully D. Bowen, Henry Lippitt, William H. Reynolds, Charles H. Merriman, Samuel Chace, and Harvey Chace, and the name of the concern was changed to "Manville Company."

The proprietorship has changed somewhat since this purchase, but the name is unaltered. Tully D. Bowen has deceased, and others have sold out, but the great bulk of the interest remains in the same names as in 1863.

The Manville Company was incorporated May, 1863. The stockholders now in the estate are T. D. Benson, John H. Taft, Anthony & Hall, H. B. Benson, Harvey Chace & Sons, R. Handy ; Harvey Chace, President ; John A. Taft, Treasurer and Agent.

At an early day, a furnace was erected here, the iron ore of Cumberland, which is now shipped to Pennsylvania, having a recognized value with such men as the Wilkinsons and those connected in business with them. Here was cast hollow ware of the various kinds needed in domestic service. The saw mill, fulling and grist mills stood where the brick mill now stands. There is a tradition that one of the kettles from the furnace being left out in the rain was filled with water which froze solid, and that Israel Wilkinson after the next day's sun had melted the ice sufficiently to allow it to be turned out, worked off the upper surface spherically so as to form an ice globe. This, by fixing an iron hoop around its centre so as to control it, he made into an ice sun glass and concentrating the rays of the sun through it into a focus, melted some iron wire. Israel and David Wilkinson were relatives of Oziel Wilkinson, of Pawtucket, and in a very considerable degree partook of his love for, and skill in, mechanical pursuits. The late Joseph Wilkinson, of Smithfield, was a cousin of the David Wilkinson, of Pawtucket, who invented the slide lathe. Joseph Wilkinson was a man of quick intellect and sound judgment. He would never engage in any manufacturing business, saying that where a difference of a quarter of a cent a yard in cloth would make or ruin a man, his capital should not be risked. He created the Hamlet meadows out of the original swamp, and arid sand. He also directed the reclamation of the land, afterwards the Manville meadows, and which Samuel F. Man, in his day took a great deal of pride in keeping up to the extreme point of fertility, which could only be done by careful irrigation.

The " Mott Dam," now a thing of the past, it having been flowed out by and for the benefit of the Manville Company, was the subject of an eleven years' law suit between Joseph Wilkinson, and Jenkins and Man. It was situated about one mile below the Hamlet village, and was nearly five feet high. John Whipple and Richard W. Greene were of counsel in the case, Whipple being for the complainant, Wilkinson, who owned the adjoining land, and Greene for Jenkins and Man. Afterwards Thomas A. Jenckes came into the case with Judge Greene and Thomas Steere as counsel for Wilkinson, and after the usual fortunes of a case, where both parties were pertinacious and all the counsel able, with judgment for the plaintiff in the Common Pleas, a reversal by the Supreme Court, a new trial and much expense and trouble, the case was finally settled by junior counsel on both sides, one at least of them never having been forgiven by his client for doing him that good service. Samuel F. Man died in 1847, Joseph Wilkinson in 1851 ; they were neighbors for years, and although opposing litigants, were quite capable each of appreciating the abilities of the other. The Blackstone flows without a ripple over " Mott Dam," and the intellectual vigor and varied information of Samuel F. Man, and the keen perceptions and cool understanding of Joseph Wilkinson, are only occasionally brought to mind in that locality where once they swayed an influence respected and acknowledged.

Thomas Mann was one of the first settlers of Smithfield, was Judge of the Court of Common Pleas, under the old system, and Town Clerk of the town of Smithfield, for many years. He was first chosen clerk in June, 1817. He was succeeded in June, 1840, by the late Gen. George L. Barnes. Stafford Mann, son of the Judge, was Town Clerk from 1850 to 1855, and was then succeeded by the present Clerk, Samuel Clark.

Stephen Clark, father of Samuel, and son of Samuel, occupied, as did his father, the estate now owned and occupied by the present Town Clerk of Smithfield. The great-grandfather of the present owner of this fine estate, was concerned in Shay's rebellion, and the grandfather, as a boy, came first to Glocester, and afterwards to Smithfield, where he was President of the Town Council in 1798. Stephen Clark was a member of the General Assembly in 1839, and a prominent man in his town.

George and Daniel Hill were land owners near Manville,

and Jesse Brown, a proprietor in Cumberland.   David Wilkinson owned a farm about a mile from Manville, and was one of the " solid men " of the town.   The enterprise evidently did not meet the anticipations of the projectors, although the losses, if any, were not such as to embarrass men of their means.

The first mill was built at Manville in 1812.   It is four stories in height, counting the attic, 100x32, shingled on the sides, and is being renewed and promises to last for years to come.   The present mill was built in 1826, of brick, and was originally 139x42, five stories high.   In 1859, thirty-two feet were added to its length, and in 1862, forty-five feet more, making it now 216x42, with an ell, added in 1859, 80x44.   At the same time turbine wheels were put in, so that there are now six stories filled with machinery.   The entire machinery has been changed since 1847, and under the superintendence of Mr. Russell Handy, who has been, with a short intermission, thirty years about the mill, everything presents a neat and improving aspect.   By purchases of real estate, and improved machinery, with other outlays, the value of the Manville property has been doubled since 1866.   The new dam, built year before last, is one of the best, if not the very finest on the river.   It is constructed of large hewn granite ; is 246 feet long ; 13 feet in width at the bottom, 8 feet on top, with cap ; 18 feet in height on the average, and rests upon solid rock its entire length.   In some places it is 24 feet in height, and composed of stones 10 to 14 feet in length, and 2 feet square.   It was commenced August 15th, 1868, and finished in three months and one day.   It cost, say $32,000.   The foundation for a new mill, 350x76, with an ell 76x36, is finished.   It is of the most solid description.   It is built of hewn granite, the stones being from 6 to 8 feet in length and 18 inch face by 12 inches in depth.   It cost some $62,000.   The work recently done on the trenches, bulkheads, &c., has cost $20,-

000 more. The fall of water is 19 feet, and the volume sufficient to drive both mills, or rather the three mills, as the old wooden structure before mentioned is to have new machinery. Three hundred hands are now employed, and the horse power, 250. The entire power is 900. The looms in use, 348; spindles, 20,000; and about four hundred tons of coal are used to heat the mill. One hundred additional looms and 4,000 spindles are to be placed in the present and old wooden mills. The mill to be erected on the new foundation is calculated for 45,000 spindles. The goods made here now are fine lawns for printing, these having taken the place of fine shirtings, which were equal in quality to the goods of the New York Mills. A thousand acres of land give the Manville Company "ample room and verge enough" for agricultural pursuits; and they have on their premises some of the finest building sites in the State. The village, which lies on the Smithfield side of the river, is well built on wide streets, shaded with beautiful maple and elm trees. It is perfectly kept and evinces the results of careful oversight. The Company is fitting up a large two-story store, and making preparations for slaughtering cattle, so as to provide plentifully and cheaply for the wants of their operatives.

For the purposes of a school house and a large hall, there is a fine two-story building, and we have rarely seen better furnished rooms than the primary and intermediate school rooms present. Leading up to this building and the church which stands beside it is a wide and pleasant avenue having noble trees on either side. Episcopal services are conducted in the church regularly, and the edifice, which will seat three hundred persons, has been cushioned, carpeted and handsomely painted by the Company. There is a good organ, and the "dim religious light" which streams in at the windows is in perfect keeping with the atmosphere of the village. No where is to be found a more quiet and thorough-

ly orderly community.   The late Samuel F. Man was a strict
disciplinarian, and he laid out Manville regularly, and maintained in it, during his life, a sober and industrious population.   The present proprietors act upon the assumption that
wealth has its duties, as well as its power and privileges, and
they are not only improving the looks and capacity of their
establishment, but they have regard to the welfare of their
operatives.   No liquor is sold in the village, and persons employed must conform to the proprieties and outward morali-
ties of life-   Mr. Handy and the Treasurer, John A. Taft,
Esq., make it evident, by every word and act, that they feel
the responsibility which, whether acknowledged or not,
presses upon all who have the direction of large numbers of
individuals.

The population of Manville is about 1,000 ; there are 100
scholars in the Sabbath school; and the district school is well
attended.   As a proof of the advance made in the character
of their manufactures, it suffices to state, that in 1866 the
numbers of the yarn spun were from 30 to 35 while now
they are from 65 to 80.   This place was for many years the
residence of Hon. Bradbury C. Hill, late Senator from Smithfield in the General Assembly, and here he laid the foundation of his fortune, working sixteen hours a day, honest labor.   When that question, which caused so wide a difference
of opinion, and in many cases worked so great an alienation
of feeling between the Law and Order men,—whether Dorr
should or should not be liberated—came to agitate the
State, Mr. Man and Mr. Hill were found on opposite sides.
Mr. Man went with Charles Jackson for liberation ; Mr. Hill
could see neither its necessity nor justice.   He had sympa-
thized with the spirit and been electrified and strengthened
by the eloquence of "Old Narragansett," and he could not
change his convictions so readily as some other men, equally
able and equally honest.   He had been in the Legislature,
and had received a renomination, but Samuel F. Man, in

14

whose employ he then was, and for many years had been, told him squarely that he should be defeated, notwithstanding his nomination, unless he would pledge himself to vote for liberation; this he would not do, and he was defeated. Without acceding to the judgment of Mr. Hill, it is, at this day, at least, refreshing to recall the political firmness of one, who even at the loss of office, carried out his own views of individual duty.

ALBION.

Samuel Clarke, who died in the year 1817, owned the Albion privilege, together with a large tract of land on the Smithfield side of the Blackstone river; and this property descended by will to his two sons, Samuel and Mowry Clarke. Samuel sold his interest in the same very soon to Mowry, who in 1822 deeded it to Samuel Hill, Jr., of Smithfield, and Abraham Wilkinson, of North Providence, who were the first to improve the water power, they having purchased land on the Cumberland side of the river, of Jotham Carpenter. (For several years the place was called Monticello.) In 1822, Hill and Wilkinson having no more than commenced operations by building a dam, Wilkinson sold to Hill his interest in the fifty-three acres of land then comprising the estate, and the water power bounding on the Pawtucket river, for the consideration of fifteen hundred dollars. March 22d, 1822, Samuel Hill sold to Joseph Harris, Preserved Arnold, Daniel G. Harris and William Harris, Abraham and Isaac Wilkinson, nine undivided tenth parts of this estate. In March, 1823, Mr. Hill sold to the last named parties his remaining tenth part, leaving the entire fee in them. This company erected in 1823 the old stone mill, about 50x100, four stories high, which is still in operation, and which contained 108 looms. In 1830, the interest of Abraham and Isaac Wilkinson and Samuel B. Harris, who had in the meantime become part owner, was sold at Sheriff's sale

by Mark Aldrich, Deputy Sheriff, at the suit of the Lime
Rock Bank, George Wilkinson, son of Abraham, being the
purchaser, the privilege at this time being known as Albion.
George Wilkinson, in 1833, the Harrises and Preserved Arnold having disposed theretofore of their interest, for the
sum of ninety thousand dollars, sold to Horace Waldo, Francis Waldo and George Trott, Jr., of the city of New York,
two undivided thirds of the Albion estate. The Waldos
and Trott sold in 1834, to William and Christopher Rhodes,
Orray Taft, Thomas Truesdell and Robert Rhodes, who
owned the entire estate, the title to which we have traced
in a general and not detailed way.

Afterwards Orray Taft sold his interest to William A.
Howard, of Providence, and Thomas Truesdell his, to
Robert Rhodes. In the year 1864, William A. Howard
deeded his interest to Harvey and Samuel B. Chace. During the few years previous to 1854, Gen. Libbeus Tourtellot,
now of Woonsocket, was superintendent, and made very
material improvements in the place, adding not only to the
value but to the beauty of the village.

In 1854, Harvey and Samuel B. Chace purchased three-
eighths of this estate, and in the year 1856, the Albion Company was incorporated by act of the General Assembly.
Afterwards, Robert Rhodes disposed of his interest to H.
and S. B. Chace, and Samuel B. Chace of his to Harvey
Chace, who transferred to the Albion Company, which then
first organized under the charter.

In 1832, a wooden mill was erected near where the station
of the Providence and Worcester railroad now stands,
35x60, which was burned in 1837. Another wooden mill
had also been built in 1830, by George Wilkinson, called
the Green mill, about 40x120, which has recently been dis-
mantled. As before stated, the original stone mill is still in
operation, and on the north is now joined by a new picker
and carding room, built of brick, two stories high, one

hundred feet in length, while on the south is the new mill, built of brick, 120x52, with the foundations laid, and wheel in for an additional hundred feet. This new mill is six stories in height, most thoroughly constructed, and has a large and commodious tower, which will be in the centre of the building when completed as planned. The entire mill will be, in round numbers, four hundred feet in length when finished. There is also a cloth room and office, constructed of brick, two stories high, 40x60 ; a blacksmith and machine shop two stories in height, brick, and in the upper story of which weaving is performed ; a saw mill 80x25 ; a two story stone store house ; and one half of the Green mill, 55x40, to be used as a store house, the other half having been transformed into an imposing tenement house. A new modern dam was erected in 1854.

As is the case with many, if not most of our manufacturing villages, Albion presents to the traveller by rail its least attractive aspect. Ineeed the village is hardly to be seen from the cars. In reality the eighty tenements are mostly situated on a high bluff overlooking the river, and are very pleasantly and even picturesquely placed. Nor is this all. Standing on the platform in front of the station, and looking north, there is as pretty a landscape as is to be found on the river. At the right, looking across the dam, is a bit of scenery which is unique and perfect. The river is placid ; the water splashes over the dam with a joyous beauty ; the rugged rocks rise rough and abruptly on the thither shore ; the graceful birches are reflected in the water below, and the light and cheerful green of the springing foliage contrasts charmingly with the dark gray of the granite ; while taking in a wider sweep, the river winds gracefully between the hills on either side, which, by their curvature, seem to mingle not far off in one mass of bright and living verdure. In the early spring-time, and when the autumn rains begin, Muzzy brook, which once turned the wheel of Oziel Wilkin-

son's forge, leaps in a succession of cascades from the meadow
above to the river below ; and, like one of Ruggles's gems,
is, in its own way, wholly unapproachable. It is infinitely
more lovely than the celebrated falls of Inversnaid, on Loch
Lomond, about which so many pretty and poetical things
have been said and sung.

In 1856, the Manville Company and the Albion Company
gave the land, and built a road between Manville and Albion,
along the river side.   In 1868, as a continuation thereof,
Messrs. Harvey and Samuel B. Chace constructed a bridge
across the Blackstone at Albion, and a road of a mile in
length to the Cumberland Hill road, to Providence. The
entire length of the road is some three miles, which together
with the bridge cost, aside from the land, not less than
ten thousand dollars, and which the towns of Smithfield and
Cumberland accepted as a public highway, paying in all to
the builders, three thousand dollars.

The fall of water at Albion is fourteen feet ; the power in
use—water—three hundred and eighty horse power; the
power available is something like eight hundred horse
power.   There are four hundred looms, and from 18 to 20,-
000 spindles in operation, there being power provided for
twenty-five thousand spindles.   Two hundred and eighty-
five hands are employed; four hundred tons of coal used per
annum ; and four million yards of print cloth produced annually.

David Alexander is the efficient superintendent of this
concern.

LONSDALE.

This place, owned by the Lonsdale Company, situated
seven miles from Providence, on the Blackstone river, was
commenced as a manufacturing village in 1829, and the first
mill was started in 1832, the second mill in the same year.

The bleaching department was put in operation in 1844. About ninety thousand yards of cloth are put in process of bleaching per day. These three mills contain 860 looms, 41,000 spindles, and the fall of water is 22 feet. The horse power is: water, 550; engine in bleachery, 180; engine supplementary to water power in summer, 250. Three thousand tons of coal are consumed annually at the bleachery ; two thousand at the mills; one thousand at the gas works. The number of hands employed is 850, and 3,200 bales of cotton, averaging 275 pounds each, are used each year. The product is five and one half million yards of fine sheetings and other goods. The girls in the finishing rooms of the fine goods, such as silesias, earn from seven to twelve dollars per week.

The population of the village is about sixteen hundred. A fine brick school house, large enough for the several departments of the public school, has been erected by the company, and the rent is given to the district. A new brick building, 62x111, is building for library and other purposes. The superintendent, Edward Kilburn, has had supervision over the establishments since 1847. Of the new mill and new village, as they are in Cumberland, we make no special mention.

VALLEY FALLS.

In April, of the year 1812, Joseph Jenks, of Smithfield, for the sum of $2,500, sold to Abraham, Isaac and David Wilkinson, sixteen acres of land, including the water privilege at Valley Falls, and gave a right of way through his land to Central Falls. In November of the same year, David Wilkinson sold his interest to Abraham and Isaac. The latter constructed the turnpike from Pawtucket to Lonsdale, at the old oak which stands in the centre of the road leading west to the village of Lonsdale. Isaac Wilkinson was an excellent mechanic, and at the age of seventeen had charge of the Cupola, now Franklin Foundry, in Providence. During the war of 1812, he cast cannon sixty days in succession, two heats per day. Abraham and Isaac Wilkinson built, about the year 1820, a stone mill, which has recently been demolished. In 1830, Henry Marchant purchased one-fourth part of the privilege. William Harris owned one-twelfth, and Crawford Allen the remainder. William Harris built, about 1820, a mill which was burned in 1830. In 1833, Crawford Allen erected the stone mill on the Cumberland side of the river. This mill, as originally built, was 44x112, and four stories in height. To it was added, by the Valley Falls Company, in 1868, an addition, of brick, two stories, 40x90 ; one, also of brick, 40x90, three stories, and a picker house, of stone, two stories, 54x40.

On the Smithfield side a wooden mill, 125x44, four stories, was erected in 1844, and a brick mill, four stories, 156x44, in 1849. These mills are now run by turbine wheels, four doing the work of eleven breast wheels. The first self-acting mules, operated on the Blackstone river, were started at Valley Falls. When the Messrs. Chace applied to Brown & Pitcher, Pawtucket, to build them, Mr. Pitcher refused to have anything to do about it; afterwards, Mr. James Brown built them. In 1868, this privilege became the property of Samuel B. Chace, and thereafter of the Valley Falls Company, of which Mr. Chace is the principal member. Since that year, improvements have been made on a large scale about the mills, and to a considerable extent in the village, mainly owned by the company, and containing a population of something like two thousand inhabitants. In the year 1852–3, the Messrs. Chace constructed a stone dam of the most substantial kind ; although not so high as that at Manville, it is one of the finest and perhaps the handsomest dam on the river, it being built upon a curve, of hewn stone, with abutments which are remarkable for their solidity.

Broad street is a quiet, pleasant street, upon which are

numerous charming residences, with ample grounds, fine trees and shrubbery, and an air of neatness and elegance which speaks well for their owners. That of Mr. Samuel B. Chace is the largest and most modern, and is surrounded by flower gardens and all the insignia of refined taste. On the opposite side of the street is a vacant lot laid down in a beautiful lawn, giving what so many seem indifferent to, but which is so important, an attractive prospect from the front windows of the dwelling. Other places are rich in grass and trees and ample space and that air of retirement, which is so grateful to the busy or the cultivated man.

The fall is, on the Cumberland side of the river, eleven feet seven inches, and on the Smithfield side fourteen feet, the gain on the Smithfield side being made by the increased length in the trench. The horse power—water—is 400; 350 hands are employed; 750 looms run, and 35,000 spindles.

Valley Falls, in Smithfield, is surpassed by no village in the State in its efforts in behalf of temperance. Not only are there frequent lectures upon the subject, but the influence of the Company and its managers is persistently exercised in favor of sobriety. For many years no place has been let by the Messrs. Chace, as none is now, for the sale of intoxicating liquors, nor is any such sale permitted on any premises owned by the Company.

CENTRAL FALLS.

We doubt if there is anywhere a more distinctive and noteworthy manufacturing village than Central Falls; one where within the same area of territory there are so many mechanics and operatives who own the houses in which they live. No one conversant with this place can have failed to notice the great number of small but comfortable houses, each with a small garden plat, which distinguishes this thriving village. It bears evident marks of thrift, comfort and independence. There have been indeed, within the few years last past, some large establishments erected, and those employed in these, like the great majority of operatives in manufacturing establishments, do not own premises of their own; but there are yet a great number of well-to-do persons, neither possessed of riches, nor dependent upon boarding houses, who form a population industrious, prudent and substantial. The business is varied; large capital is employed; the streets are well graded and curbed; and activity and public spirit prevail.

The first intimation we have of the use of the water of the Blackstone river at Central Falls was that Benjamin Jenks erected a snuff mill near the dividing line between the towns of Smithfield and North Providence, and got his power by extending a trench by the side of the river up stream, into the river, which was the usual way of utilizing the water of the Blackstone. At what time this business was abandoned is uncertain.

The next intimation we have is that Stephen Jenks (great-grandfather of the present Stephen A. and Alvin F. Jenks), bought, in 1763, of Gideon Jenks and Ezekiel Carpenter, three-fourths of an acre, on which was built the trip-hammer and blacksmith shop, which was afterwards known as the blacksmith shop lot, and is now owned by the mill owners of Central Falls. Whether Stephen Jenks utilized the water of the Blackstone previous to the erection of the dam by Charles Keene, in 1780, is not known. Captain James S. Brown thinks there was no use of the water previous to the building of Keene's dam, in 1780.

In 1777 William Jenks, of Wrentham, Mass., sold a lot of land, comprising some ten acres, located near the old dam at Central Falls, to Benjamin Cozzens, of Providence (clothier), who had a fulling mill at Pawtucket Falls, which

15

was carried away in the great freshet of 1807. Benjamin
Cozzens was the father of Benjamin Cozzens, the lawyer, of
Providence, whose daughter is the wife of Abraham Payne,
Esq., of Providence. This purchase from William Jenks
was evidently made for the purpose of using the water
power for his business.

In 1780 Benjamin Cozzens sold to Charles Keene that
portion of this estate purchased of William Jenks as now
includes the Stafford Manufacturing Company's mill estate,
stone house and blacksmith shop lot, Chocolate Mill lot and
the dam lot, so called.

Charles Keene built the first dam across the river at Central Falls, and perhaps the first dam across the Blackstone
anywhere. The dam was built for Mr. Keene by Sylvanus
Brown, father of Capt. James S. Brown, of Pawtucket.
Keene erected a building for the manufacture of scythes
and other edge tools, and was called an edge tool manufacturer. A part of the building was occupied by a man
named Wheat, for the manufacture of chocolate, which
gave the name of Chocolate Mills to the village, and it retained that name down to 1824.

In 1784 Keene sold one-third of the estate to Levi Hall,
merchant, of Providence. At this time (1784), Keene &
Hall owned the whole water power at Central Falls, although there are intimations in the deed from Gideon Jenks
and Ezekiel Carpenter to Stephen Jenks of the three-fourths
acre lot, and also in the deed of Cozzens to Keene, reserving
one-third of three-fourths of an acre, but as has been said
before, it is not found that any water power was used previous to 1780 and before the building of Keene's dam.

In 1796 Anna Keene, widow of Charles, sold to Stephen
Jenks, Stephen Jenks, Jr., and Moses Jenks, two-thirds of
the Keene & Hall estate, and in 1806, Sarah Hall, widow
of Levi Hall, sold to Stephen Jenks one third of the Keene
& Hall lot. On the three-fourths acre lot, by Jenks in 1763,

afterwards known as the blacksmith shop lot, was built the trip hammer and blacksmith shop, in which were manufactured iron ship bolts and other ship work, the ship anchors being made by Stephen Jenks and Oziel Wilkinson, of Pawtucket.

The water power, in 1806, was principally owned by Stephen Jenks, including the blacksmith shop lot and the Keene estate. The Keene building, called the Chocolate Mill, was, in 1807 or 1808, owned and occupied by the Smithfield Manufacturing Company, and used for the manufacture of cotton yarns. In this mill, about 1812, and after, were employed Anthony, Eliza, Alexander, Isaiah and Richard B. Gage and others. Their office and place of putting up their yarns was in Pawtucket, Mass., near where the Congregational Church now stands. It is said the Company, with their small amount of machinery—400 spindles,—suffered more from the lack of water than 40,000 spindles do now.

In 1811 Stephen Jenks made a contract with the United States Government to manufacture 10,000 muskets for $11.50 apiece. He erected a building to finish the guns in, part of which was afterwards used by Stephen Jenks & Sons for a machine shop, and the balance for the manufacture of cotton cloth. This building was burned in January, 1829, and was on the site of what was afterwards the Duck Mill, built by Lemuel H. Arnold and Palemon Walcott, for the manufacture of cotton duck.

In 1832 Charles Moies and George F. Jenks bought the Duck Mill estate, and the mill was occupied by Moies, Ingraham & Co., for the manufacture of cotton thread, the firm consisting of Charles Moies, H. N. Ingraham, Benjamin F. Greene and Samuel Saunders. The lot on which the mill stood was sold, many years afterwards, to Rufus Stafford, and is now part of the Stafford Manufacturing Company's estate.

In 1823 the owners of the water power at Central Falls had their property platted and divided into separate water privileges, numbered from one to six inclusive, which were apportioned among the owners according to their ownership, which appears on the records of the town of Smithfield. Each privilege was to have an aperture in the side of the trench six feet long and two feet below the top of the dam, making the aggregate length of the apertures thirty-six feet and two feet deep below the top of the dam, which, it was considered, would be the full capacity of the river at that time. The apertures have since been increased to one hundred and fifty-six feet in length and sixteen inches deep.

Lot and privilege No. 1 was bought by John Kennedy, and a brick mill erected for the manufacture of cotton cloth in 1825. It afterwards went into the hands of Wm. Jenkins, of Providence, from him to John Gardner and others, and from them to Rufus Stafford and others, and now belongs to the Stafford Manufacturing Company.

In 1824 a mill was built upon privilege No. 2 by David and George Jenks. Upon the completion of this the mill and the Central Falls bridge were dedicated. There was a foot-bridge built previous to this time. It was a gala day for the village. The meeting was held in one of the rooms of the mill, and attended by nearly all the inhabitants of the village, men, women and children, and a large number from Pawtucket, where some of the principal owners of the village resided. James C. Starkweather, of Pawtucket, was the orator of the day. After speeches were made and toasts drank, Stephen Jenks arose from his seat and proclaimed that the village should be named Central Falls, which was received with clapping of hands, stamping of feet and swinging of hats and bonnets. The meeting held until 12 o'clock at night. It was a moonlight night, and at that hour the citizens of Pawtucket who had attended the meeting, were seen wending their way over Central Hill towards Pawtucket, some on their feet and others in the roughest part of the way on their hands and knees. There is no record that they did not all arrive safely home the next morning. There were anxious enquiries made by their wives during the night, however, for their absent husbands in Pawtucket.

The lower story of this mill was occupied by Simmons L. Hale and William Havens for the manufacture of cotton threads, and afterwards by Uriah Benedict and George F. Jenks for the manufacture of threads. The balance of the mill was occupied by the owners for the manufacture of cotton cloth. Afterwards the mill estate was divided by the Court—one-half to Andrew Jenks, son of George, and the other half to the representatives of David Jenks. H. N. Rogers and James Dennis bought the David Jenks part, which they have since sold to the Stafford Manufacturing Company, and is now a part of their estate. The other part of the estate is still owned by Andrew Jenks.

Privilege No. 3 was bought by the Pawtucket Thread Manufacturing Company, consisting of Jabal Ingraham, Bosworth Walker, William Allen and Uriah Benedict. The present stone mill was built by them in 1825. The lower story was occupied by Fields & Jacobs for the manufacture of machinery, the two upper stories by Dwight Ingraham for the manufacture of cotton cloth, and the balance of the mill by the Company for the manufacture of threads. The estate is now owned, three-fourths by the heirs of Stephen Benedict, and one-fourth by the heirs of Bosworth Walker.

The north half of privilege No. 4 was bought by Stephen Benedict and Joseph Wood, on which they built a wooden mill, in 1840, for the manufacture of cotton cloth, and is now owned by the estate of Stephen Benedict, and at present leased by the firm of Thurber, Horton & Wood.

The south half of No. 4 and the north half of No. 5 privileges were bought by Alvin Jenks and David G. Fales, on which they built a wooden mill in 1835. The lower story was occupied by them for the manufacture of machinery, and the other part of the mill was let to parties for the manufacture of cotton goods. The estate was sold by them to Phetteplace & Seagraves, on which they have built a large brick mill for the manufacture of woolen goods, and now known as the Central Falls Woolen Mill.

The south half of No. 5 privilege was bought by Charles Moies, John Moies and George F. Jenks, and in 1839 they built a wooden mill, a part of which was occupied by themselves for the manufacture of cotton cloth, a part by H. N. Ingraham for the manufacture of print cloths, and the basement by David Martin for the manufacture of spools and bobbins. Afterwards it was occupied by Greene & Daniels for twenty years in the manufacture of cotton thread and yarn, and has since been sold to the Pawtucket Hair Cloth Company, who now own it.

Privilege No. 6 was owned by Stephen Jenks. In 1826 he purchased the meeting house of the Universalist Society of Attleboro', Mass., removed it to this privilege, and in 1827 converted it into a mill for the manufacture of cotton cloth. This mill, in 1830, was sold by his assignee to Jas. F. Simmons, Lemuel H. Arnold and Ruel Richards, who made large additions to it. The lower story was occupied by Fales & Jenks for the manufacture of machinery, and the balance of the mill by the owners for the manufacture of cotton cloth. In 1837 Arnold sold to Charles Moies his part of the estate. In 1846 the whole estate was sold to Joseph and Samuel Wood, and upon the death of Samuel Wood was bought by Joseph Wood and John A. Adams, and by them sold to the Pawtucket Hair Cloth Company, who now own the estate. The old mill building was sold to Weatherhead & Thompson, and by them moved south several hundred feet, where it now stands. It is at present used by them as a tannery, for the manufacture of leather belting, etc.

THOMAS D. RICE & COMPANY,

manufacturers of wooden jewelry, curtain fixtures, chairs, and of every variety of goods turned in wood. This is the only concern in the country where wooden jewelry is made. At first blush, one would hardly suppose that an article of this kind would appeal very strongly to an esthetic taste, or meet with a large demand. But a little reflection suffices to recall the fact that those who cannot afford diamonds, nor coral, nor gold, nor yet shell ornaments, are still as fond as the rich of whatever is convenient, graceful and fashionable. The belles and beaux of the rural districts; the young men and ruddy maidens of the villages, who are compelled to economy in expenditure for personal adornments, imitate as far and as nearly as they can those more favored with this world's goods, and display quite as insatiable a desire for external embellishments. And in regard to the articles under consideration, as in respect to much more showy and costly trinkets, it may be said in the language of the poet, that "things are not what they seem." Many an apparent diamond, which to the uninitiated eye appears a gem of purest ray serene, is nothing but paste; many a pretended pearl, is but glass; and many a chain of ostensible gold, in lengthened links of glittering metal, long drawn out, is simply brass within, and a film of gold without. And so we shall rightly expect that our sylvan jewelry will betray no glimpse of wood.

Of course the work is done by machinery. Five thousand sleeve buttons are turned out in a day, and breast pins and other articles in like proportion. These are then enameled; some in gay single colors; some in variegated hues; and some in black. These latter are a useful and tasteful article for every day wear as sleeve or dress buttons; neat, unobtrusive and admirably adapted to sedate attire. Nor should we forget to mention the cheap and handsome rosaries upon which the unlettered Catholic may tell her prayers, with as true a devotion and as spiritual a fervor as animates her educated sister in perusing the illuminated page of her gold-clasped missal.

This concern has been in operation only one year, and yet its orders for children's chairs range from one to five thousand, and for certain kinds of jewelry from one gross to two barrels. It uses five horse power of water, and, in dry seasons, a ten horse power engine, and employs five hands. It is certainly a curiosity and exhibits most conspicuously Yankee ingenuity and Yankee enterprise.

In 1830 DAVID G. FALES and ALVIN JENKS formed a co-partnership for the manufacture of cotton machinery, and commenced business in this place in a hired shop. Their first piece of work was a spooler, made for a firm in Richmond, Virginia, for which they received $60. In 1833 they purchased the right to manufacture in Rhode Island Hubbard's Patent Rotary Pump. The first ring spinning frames were made by this firm in 1845; the first ring twisters, being among the first of these machines built in this country, for thread, worsted and silk, were made by them, in 1846, for Benjamin Greene. Several years since, Fales, Jenks & Sons made for and sent to J. & P. Coats, the celebrated manufacturers of " Coats " sewing thread, at Paisley, Scotland, nine twisters, dressers and winders. In 1859–60 they built a furnace for castings, and in 1861 enlarged their operations very considerably. In 1862–3 they erected a brick shop, three stories high, 300x63, with an ell 70x60, which was afterwards sold to the American Linen Company. In 1866 they removed their works to Pawtucket, whither we follow them only to say that they still added to the variety and importance of their business.

WEATHERHEAD, THOMPSON & CO.,

Manufacture oak tanned leather belting, and patent lace and picker leather. They commenced business in 1858, in a couple of buildings aggregating 70x20 feet. Their first year's sales amounted to twenty thousand dollars. This year (1870), they received the diploma of the Rhode Island Society for the Encouragement of Domestic Industry, and their annual sales amount to $200,000. They occupy a building 110x40, built of wood, five stories high; one 100x 28 feet; one of brick, 70x30 feet, two stories in height; use an engine of 70 horse power, and employ 35 hands. They also manufacture all kinds of spools for silk and cotton thread, employing in this department 15 hands.

M. B. ARNOLD & CO.,

Manufacturers of plain and fancy confectionery, occupy a building 67x30 feet, built of wood, two and a half stories high. They employ sixteen hands, keep two double teams constantly on the road, and their annual sales amount to nearly one hundred thousand dollars.

PAWTUCKET HAIR CLOTH COMPANY.

This concern has grown out of the persevering efforts of a few individuals to establish a novel and difficult industry. In the last completed edition of the Encyclopædia Britannica it is stated that: "In the manufacture of hair cloth, either plain or damasked, the weaver uses a sort of hook shuttle, which he passes between the threads of the warp or shed, towards his left hand; the assistant, or server, places a single hair over the hook, and the weaver draws it through the warp. The placing of the hairs one by one renders this a tedious operation, *and one that does not admit of the application of machinery*, which is so advan-

16

tageously employed in fabrics where the shot or weft consists of a continuous thread."

And this statement is in accordance with the present state of manufacture abroad. There, two hands are required for each loom, and these looms are of the most cumbrous character, resembling the old fashioned hand looms, which, in the last century, were to be found in almost every New England farmer's household.

So novel an industry is entitled to a brief space. To begin at the beginning. The hair used is that of horses' tails, and is imported from South America and Russia, mostly from the latter country. It is purchased at the great annual fairs of Isbilt and Nijni Nooyorod. That purchased in June at the latter place will be received in about sixty days; and that bought at Isbilt, in February, in about six months. As it comes in various colors, it is, for the purposes of this concern, all dyed black. A certain proportion, however, is purchased in England and France, already prepared for the loom. It is worth from fifty cents to four dollars per pound, according to length, the price increasing in rapid ratio after the length attains twenty-four inches.

The "rough hair," or that which is imported in its natural state, is hackled, and the shortest sold to the manufacturers of mattresses, it being first curled. After being hackled, the different lengths are combed out, assorted, tied in bunches, and ready for coloring. After this process, the bunches are carefully inspected, measured, and put away for the loom. The cloth is made in widths of from fourteen to thirty-two inches.

Contrary to the popular idea, the hair is not, as a rule, round. A section under the microscope shows a form as though a third of a circle had been cut off, and the flat portion slightly indented. This conformation caused some difficulties in the manipulation, which required great skill and the most delicate machinery to overcome. The warp used is made of cotton, and prepared with great care. A bunch of hair which has been soaked in water is placed in position, and the individual hairs are picked up, to be by the shuttle laid carefully in the weft. If the machine fails to take a hair, which occasionally happens at the first trial, it continues its efforts until it succeeds, the other portions of the machinery standing still in the meantime. The shuttle is an awkward looking, but most delicately operating implement. The hair must not be bruised, and it must not be stretched; the necessity for such gentle manipulation led to the idea embodied in the Encyclopædia, that no machinery could be constructed capable of performing the operation with sufficient exactitude and regularity. It is impossible to appreciate this loom without seeing it in operation, and having the benefit of the explanations of its ingenious inventor, Mr. Isaac Lindsley, who has been many years at work upon it, and who, after surmounting obstacles which would have been insuperable to one less tenacious and skillful, has brought it to what to the common comprehension seems perfection. The precision of the loom will be seen when we state that one girl attends ten of them.

It will be readily understood that a manufacture of this kind has not grown up in a day, and that almost every process has required new inventions in order not only to cheapness and excellence of production, but to any product. Thus, in shearing by hand the cloth to get rid of the ends of hairs, which, more or less, would be found sticking up in the surface, it was impossible always to perform the work as rapidly as was necessary. Mr. Lindsley therefore invented an apparatus which takes the place of twenty-five girls, and answers the purpose completely. It is overlooked by a girl who earns a dollar and a half a day, without manual exertion save of the slightest character, but who gives the machine strict attention to see that it receives no impediment from clogging or otherwise. The finishing of the cloth is the same as in the manufacture of woolen goods —with differences. The quality of the cloth is better than that made by hand, but it comes in the market in competition with that made where twenty-five cents a day is ordinary wages. In Germany the awkward hand looms are found in the peasants' homes, and whatever the children earn by working them is so much gain.

In 1864 this company erected the spacious building in Central Falls, now occupied by it. It is built of brick, 204x54 feet, four stories in height, with an additional basement story under one-half its length, with an ell 75x24 feet, four stories. It is operated by water—90 horse power ; 100 hands are employed, and 400 looms are run. Eventually 525 looms will be put in. Three thousand five hundred yards of hair cloth are made per month.

The girls who tend the looms earn, on an average, nearly a dollar and fifty cents per day. To Gen. Arnold, the treasurer, is due great credit for the conduct of the business in its earlier days, and to Mr. Lindsley the praise of a perseverance which knew no flagging, and a fertility of resource which surmounted every difficulty. The various inventions of Mr. Lindsley are patented as well in England, France and Germany as in this country, and there is no reason to doubt that in his case his labors will receive a generous reward, a fate which too many inventors have never enjoyed.

THE CENTRAL FALLS WOOLEN MILL.

The company was incorporated January, 1870, but is not yet organized. Phetteplace & Seagrave, of Providence, and James L. Pierce are the owners.

The building is of brick, very substantially built, 150x50 feet, four stories high, with an ell, constructed of wood, 81x88 feet, with basement, 88x38 feet. The boiler house is of brick, 50x30 feet. Water power is used, the capacity being 50 horse power, and is to be supplemented, when the mill is filled with machinery, by an engine. This mill is just starting up with 24 broad looms, and six setts of cards. The product is to be cassimeres and doeskins. The full capacity of the mill is fourteen setts.

Mr. Pierce is a practical manufacturer, having been with Edward Harris, of Woonsocket, for some fifteen years, and a member of the manufacturing firm of J. T. Seagrave & Company, (Granite Woolen Company,) Burrillville. He will have the charge of the mill, and will make a medium and fine quality of goods, having introduced all the newest and most improved machinery. With the capital of the old-established firm in Providence, and the skill and energy of Mr. Pierce, success is not doubtful.

THE STAFFORD MANUFACTURING COMPANY

make white and colored soft enameled spool thread, for hand and machine sewing. This company was incorporated in 1864, with a capital of $300,000. It is named in honor of the late Rufus J. Stafford, who originated the business in 1859, raised it to about one-half its present dimensions, and died in 1863. The organization is as follows:

John A. Adams, of Central Falls, President and Agent.
Joseph Wood, of Central Falls, Treasurer.
John A. Taft, of Providence, Secretary.

The premises occupied by this company are situated on the west side of the Blackstone River, and consist of a very ·eligible lot of land and two mills, with the requisite buildings. Very great improvements have been made, and are now making. One mill is stone, 102x40, three stories high, and was formerly used for the manufacture of cotton cloth, the company owning one-half. The other mill was built in

1824, of brick, and was originally about half its present size. It is now 204x40 feet, and five stories high. The dye house is also of brick, 60x30 feet; an addition to the mill has been made by the present company, of brick, 140x30 feet, three stories high, and one of the same material, 70x36 feet, four stories high. The store house is of stone, 60x30 feet, two stories in height.

This mill was erected by John Kennedy and Almy & Brown, was afterwards owned by John Gardner, then by Stafford & Wood, and finally passed into the hands of the present owners. When in full operation this concern pays about $2,000 per month for spools, and about $5,000 per year for printing labels, &c. Every spool of thread is inspected before it is packed, and the number of yards warranted is conscientiously given. The girls who wind the thread earn from $1 to $1.25 per day. The work is of course light, requiring rather care and dexterity than severe labor. The establishment is evidently managed with that judgment and scrutinizing care which are essential to success in so large a concern.

The number of spindles is 13,000; 25,000 dozen spools of thread are manufactured per week; about 300 hands are employed; the pay roll is $6,500 per month; the water power used is 300-horse power; 500 tons of coal are consumed per annum, and 500,000 pounds of cotton.

The President, Mr. Adams, is a thoroughly practical manufacturer, having begun at the beginning and witnessed and made the business as it has grown in magnitude and the excellence of its product. Competent to superintend the mills, and manage the out-of-door affairs of this extensive manufacture, it is not surprising that this company should stand in the front rank in its own line of trade.

It is always as pleasant as it is instructive to meet one who, fully conversant with an important branch of business, is yet willing to communicate general information respecting it to those who are in pursuit of knowledge. Abernethy was a very great physician, but an unchancy man to interrogate largely. We are indebted to Mr. Adams for the pleasure of a good deal more than a merely formal interview, and for ideas concerning topics of a wider scope than his immediate personal interest.

C. C. Holland, manufacturer of cotton yarns, began business in 1867, in company with A. A. Stafford. He now occupies the Andrew Jencks Mill, so-called, which is built of stone, is 40x90 feet, three stories in height, and uses 30-horse power of water, taken from the Blackstone River. The mill contains 2,500 spindles, employs 22 hands, and consumes 2,500 pounds of cotton per week.

Thurber, Horton & Wood are manufacturers of light sheetings, print cloths, threads and yarns. They occupy a stone mill erected in 1824 by Uriah Benedict, Bosworth Walker and William Allen. It is a very substantial and handsome structure, 78x44 feet, four stories high, with an ell of brick, 28x16 feet. Another mill occupied by this firm is a wooden building, 82x32 feet, three stories in height, and other room. The entire power used is water—115 horse-power. They run 7,800 spindles, 125 looms, and employ 125 hands, turning out 800 pounds of thread per day ; use 270,000 pounds of fine cotton yearly, and the annual value of their product is $125,000.

Cushman & Fuller employ 14 hands, 24 rotary knitting frames, and their annual sales are from $12,000 to $15,000 per annum.

E. L. Slocum commenced business in 1867, employs 25 hands, makes 1,100 cases of boots and shoes per year, and his annual sales amount to from $45,000 to $50,000.

E. L. FREEMAN'S PRINTING HOUSE.

The establishment of Hon. E. L. Freeman is not only

creditable to the village, but to the State. He publishes the first and only newspaper published in the town of Smithfield, and both in the size of his sheet and the quality of his arti cles his paper compares favorably with older establishments. Mr. Freeman is a practical man, who has as well the interests of the community at heart as the building up of his individual fortune. His job printing establishment is something extraordinary for a rural village, and a look through it interested us much.

Among other things we were much struck by the lithographic printing, or printing from stone, and, as many are not acquainted with the process, we will give a brief description of it. The art of printing on stone was discovered about the beginning of the present century by Alois Senefelder, an actor, of Munich, Bavaria. Differing from all other methods of printing, the impressions are obtained (by strict attention to chemical affinity) from a level surface. The stone used is a sort of calcareous slate found only in Germany, and is prepared for use by grinding and polishing the stone until it attains a perfectly smooth surface, when the design is put upon it for printing. The ink used is different from other printing inks, having a much larger proportion of greasy substances for which the stone has an affinity, while it repels or throws off water.

The design having been placed upon the stone, the printer dampens the surface of the stone with water from a sponge, which of course will not take, where the design is, from the simple fact that oil and water will not mix. A roller made of French calfskin, covered with ink, is now passed over the stone, and, while it puts ink on the design or parts intended to be printed, will not even soil the parts of the stone which are damp. A sheet of paper is then put over it and it is passed through the press and an impression obtained.

We were shown some very superior work of this description, scarcely to be distinguished from printing on steel plate,

except by an expert; in fact, many jobs are transferred from
steel plate to stone, and look nearly or quite as well.   Mr.
Freeman has the largest establishment of this kind in the
State—in fact there is but one other—and showed us sam-
ples of printing for several of the largest manufacturing
concerns within our borders, which was done in New York
or Boston before he started this enterprise; also some very
fine specimens of checks and notes.   He has nine lithographic presses, six of which are in constant operation ; and
we were certainly surprised to find so complete and well-
furnished shop in a country village, and there can certainly
be no need for our citizens to go to New York or Boston for
work ·of this kind when it can be done equally as well in
our own State, and at the same time tend to build up a
home industry.

ALLENVILLE.

Major William Smith was the first settler at this locality,
it 1703.   In 1813 the late Governor Philip Allen purchased
land of Esek Smith, a descendant of Major William Smith,
and erected a small cotton mill, which has received several
additions.   In 1857 Governor Allen sold to Earl P. Mason,
Henry Lippitt and others, and it passed, in 1867, into the
ownership of the Smithfield Manufacturing Company.   In
1820 Governor Allen built a house for the public schools,
and for religious worship on Sundays.   In 1849 the citizens
erected a schoolhouse.   In 1851 Governor Allen built a
house for public worship and gave it to the citizens of the
village.   The population is about 200.

GREENVILLE.

This village was named in honor of Major-General
Nathaniel Greene.   Resolved Waterman settled here in
1689.   Joshua Winsor had a tract of land laid out to him

17

by the town of Providence in 1685. The hotel was built by Resolved Waterman in 1733. There are three mills—, the Winsor Mills and two others. Two are woolen mills, comprising 15 sets of machinery, with two falls, aggregating 45 feet. When running, 200 hands were employed, and 420,000 yards of cloth were manufactured annually. They are now idle. Here was the pest house, in which were placed the small-pox patients at the time inoculation was introduced, prior to the Revolutionary war. In the town records of that time will be found frequent mention of this house, which was owned by Captain Andrew Waterman, and is still standing. A Baptist Church was erected here in 1701; the Free Baptist in 1821, and the Episcopal Church in 1855. The National Exchange Bank, located here, has a capital of $150,000, and the Smithfield Savings Bank deposits to the amount of $288,641.77. There is also in this place a large establishment for the manufacture of heavy team wagons. The population is nearly 1,000.

SPRAGUEVILLE.

This place was first settled by Abraham Smith, in 1733, and a grist mill was erected some years after and two houses built. About 1824 Captain Thomas Sprague purchased the privilege and erected a mill. This property afterwards came into the possession of Wanton Vaughan and others. The company is now called the Granite Mill Company. There are in operation 112 looms, 5,000 spindles. The mill is built of stone, and is 120x80 feet, with a fall of 19 feet.

Adjoining the Granite Mill estate is the Mountain Dale Hosiery Mill, owned by J. P. & J. G. Ray.

STILLWATER.

Daniel Smith located here in 1733. In 1824 Israel Arnold and his brother Welcome bought land of Daniel

Smith's descendants and erected a small cotton mill. Afterwards this property passed into the hands of Joseph Clark, of Johnston, who sold it to Robert Joslin. This mill was burned down and rebuilt several times. In 1866 Edward W. Brown purchased the property, and, with others, built a fine woolen mill and a model village—it being known as the "Stillwater Woolen Mill Co.;" chartered in 1867. The first mill of this company was burned down. The present structure is a very fine one. It is a 10-set mill, making fancy cassimeres, built of brick, and is 130x52 feet, with one ell 40x65 and one 45x32, and is five stories in height. The fall is 22 feet, affording 100 horse-power, and has steam power of nearly equal force. It employs 175 hands, and 600,000 pounds of wool are manufactured annually, making 450,000 yards of cloth. The village is neat, the tenements commodious, and supplied with pure water, and everything pertaining to the establishment is pleasant. It is, in fact, a most conspicuous testimony to what wealth, directed by taste and business capacity, can accomplish.

GEORGIAVILLE.

Thomas Owen was the first resident in this place, in 1752. James Angell and Elisha Smith built houses in the vicinity in 1700. In 1755 John Farnum and two of his sons, Joseph and Noah, came from Uxbridge, Mass., and purchased of Thomas Owen his house and land, and commenced the business of blacksmithing, having also a forge just below the present mills of the Bernon Manufacturing Company. · The iron ore was brought from Cranston, charcoal being used for smelting it. In 1760 John Farnum added to his house, which is still standing, in good repair, in possession of his granddaughter, Mrs. Ephraim Whipple. Joseph Farnum built a house here in 1770.

GEORGIAVILLE, IN SMITHFIELD, AND THE BERNON MANUFACTORY.

The village of Georgiaville owes its origin and name to the construction of a cotton mill in that locality by the "Georgia Cotton Manufacturing Company," in the year 1813.

The original company, composed of Samuel Nightingale, Samuel G. Arnold and Thomas Thompson, built a stone mill, 80x36 feet, on a fall of 18 feet of the waters of the Woonasquatucket River. They placed therein 1,000 spindles, without looms, the power loom not having been introduced into common use in Rhode Island until the year 1817.

The yarn was spun and dyed at the mill, and made into webs, which were put out to be woven by hand-loom weavers in various parts of New England.

As this was one of the pioneer mills early established in Rhode Island, a retrospective glance at the records of this old establishment will disclose the primitive state of the cotton manufacture at its commencement there, and also serve to show the contrast between the present improved processes and those of past days.

The cotton was at first picked by hand, and was distributed over the country in small parcels, to be cleaned of seeds and motes by industrious housewives and their children gathered around the domestic fireside. The loose cotton in their laps sometimes took fire, and accounts of burning up parcels of cotton, and also the dresses and houses of the industrious cotton pickers, sometimes formed a part of the business correspondence.

The price paid for hand-picking the cotton was about as much as a manufacturer now expects to obtain as the net profit for the labor of spinning it.

Equally remarkable was the price once paid for weaving yard-wide sheetings, which, as fixed by the tariff rate for No. 20 yarn, as printed on one of the old weaver's tickets, appears to have been 13 cents per yard. This is the present selling price of similar cloth. For weaving ginghams the fixed price was 1 cent additional per yard for every different color.

Another building of stone, 80x40 feet, was built in 1828, and a third addition of the same extent in 1846.

The first power looms were introduced, in 1819, by Mr. Gilmore, from England, and a receipt signed by him for a contribution of $50 is evidence of the small remuneration he received from a few manufacturers for his very useful labors.

After the power loom was introduced, in 1819, the manufacture of ginghams was superseded by that of sheetings. The number of spindles was gradually increased from 1,000, in the year 1813, to 7,700 in 1853, when the estate passed into the hands of Zachariah Allen.

With only the small number of 1,000 spindles it appears, by the records of the stoppages for want of water in the year 1822, during the extraordinary drought of that year, there were 47½ days loss of time. The Blackstone River was correspondingly low that year. This extraordinary dry season demonstrated the necessity of resorting to an artificial supply of water from reservoirs for retaining the floods of winter to swell the scanty summer streams. The first act of incorporation in New England, for the special purpose of constructing reservoirs for the supply of mills in seasons of drought, originated with the mill owners on the Woonasquatucket River in the year 1822.

The recent stoppages of mills in New England by a want of water, and the great loss to unemployed laborers resulting therefrom during several months past, now imparts a revived interest in the construction of new reservoirs to provide against a recurrence of this evil.

For this special reason a statement of what has been accomplished on the Woonasquatucket River may afford pro-

fitable information to encourage mill owners on other streams
to " go and do likewise."

Reservoirs on the Head Waters of the Woonasquatucket River.

	Acres.	Average depth.	Superficial acres, 1 foot deep.
The Greenville reservoir, constructed in 1822, contains	153	10	1.530
The Waterman reservoir, constructed in 1837, contains	318	9	2.862
The Thomas Sprague reservoir, constructed in 1830, contains	95	13 and 7	.815
Hawkins' reservoir	30	10	.300
Bernon Mill Pond, 1853	133	3	.399
Other mill ponds about	150	2	.300
Acres land	879	Water acres..	6.196

The capacity of these reservoirs is sufficient for the stor-
age of a supply of water for the mills below them during
four months, the fall being nearly 200 feet of descent to
Olneyville.

The public benefit derived from these reservoirs is mani-
fest in the fact that the increased water power thus rendered
available has proved sufficient for operating additional machinery that furnishes employment to about 2,000 more
people who directly or indirectly gain a living thereby.
Thus a few hundred acres of swamp lands, flowed artificially
as reservoirs, contribute more to the wealth and population
of Rhode Island than would several thousand acres of the
best lands of the fertile regions of the West.

In constructing the dam and the waterfall at this village
a safe plan has been adopted for the security of the work
by turning the descending floods upon a ledge of rocks on
the river side in successive cascades over the cliffs.

By artificial improvements of the water in raising the dam
to double the waterfall to 35 feet, and by the additional supply of water stored in the reservoirs, 15,000 spindles have

been operated without interruption by droughts for three years past, until the droughts of last autumn. This is certainly a remarkable contrast with eight weeks' of stoppage, caused by drought, with only 1,000 spindles in operation in 1822.

One of the principal objects of interest here is the system adopted for transmitting the motive power by belts, moving with extraordinarily swift velocities, combined with the use of light hollow shafting, made of turned and polished gas pipes, and without any pulleys thereon for belting off.

All the cards, drawing frames and fly frames contained on one floor of the mill, (250x70 feet,) and nearly 300 looms contained in the room above, of the same dimensions, are belted from only three lines of shafting extended the whole length of the mill. The belts all appear clinging around the naked shafts, and diverging both upward through the floor above and downward to the numerous machines below the shafting. Nearly every foot of their length is occupied by a belt.

This novel plan of swiftly moving belts and swiftly revolving light hollow shafting has been described as follows, in compliance with repeated requests for information: The hollow or tubular shafts are made 2¾ inches in diameter and 18 feet long, and connected by ring couplings screwed together. The weight is 5½ pounds to each foot in length, being about one-fifth of the weight of the solid shafting commonly used with their heavy plate couplings, bolts and pulleys.

To impart the same velocity to the belts used on their naked surfaces, as when pulleys are employed, it is manifestly necessary to cause them to revolve with a correspondingly increased velocity, which has been found to be about threefold faster, being about 600 revolutions per minute, while the heavy solid shafting with pulleys make about 200 revolutions per minute.

This three-fold increase of velocity increases the friction in the same ratio, while the five fold greater weight of the solid heavy shafts and pulleys correspondingly increases the friction, so that the result shows a saving of friction of two-fifths in favor of the light hollow shafting as a saving of motive power.

As the light shafts make 600 revolutions to do the same work that the common solid shafting accomplishes by 200 revolutions the immediate stress is sub-divided and reduced in the ratio of 6 to 2. The receiving pulleys require to be only one-third as large on the swiftly revolving light shaft-ing, as on the slower revolving solid shafting, while there are no driving pulleys used. An increase of speed of any machine is readily effected by winding a piece of belt leather around the shaft. The circulation of the air within and through the whole length of the hollow shafts keeps them cool. The cost of the light shafting is also much less than that of solid shafting with faced and turned couplings and pulleys.

In regard to the velocity of motion of the main driving belts the speed of a mile a minute has been adopted as a safe and advantageous rule. This may appear to be some-what dangerous for practical use; but when it is considered that ponderous English locomotive engines, weighing 35 tons or more, fly over the rigid railroad bars, and around curves, with the calculated speed of a mile a minute, and that car-loads of passengers trust themselves to be whirled over regions of country at this rate of speed the doubter may smile at the idea of hazard in trusting a pliable leather belt to travel with the same speed on its smooth and regular course.

With the velocity of a mile per minute the tension on a belt is reduced to only $6\frac{1}{4}$ pounds in transmitting 1 horse-power, and 250 pounds tension for transmitting 40 horse-power. With 6,000 feet velocity the tension is reduced to only $5\frac{1}{2}$ pounds for 1 horse-power.

To calculate the tension imposed on a leather belt for the transmission of any given horse-power it is only necessary to divide the standard measure of a horse-power, viz.: 33,000 pounds lifted 1 foot high per minute by the proposed number of feet assigned as the velocity for the belt. With 33,000 feet velocity per minute of a belt the tension would be only 1 pound for transmitting 1 horse-power; and, on the contrary, with 1 foot velocity per minute the tension would be increased to 33,000 pounds for transmitting 1 horse-power.

A belt or bridle of good leather of an inch width will sustain a weight of 1,000 pounds; but the adhesion of it to the surface of pulleys is limited to 40 or 50 pounds tension, while it operates with proper slackness to prevent straining it tightly to impair its durability. With the velocity of a mile per minute a leather belt of 6 inches width, at 40 pounds tension to the inch, will durably transmit about 40 horse-power. With a velocity of 6,000 feet per minute a main belt of 12 inches width has served to transmit the power of two water wheels, each 19 feet long and 18 feet diameter, with 16 feet fall of water, during a period of more than twelve years, and still remains serviceable. Another belt of 8 inches width has operated 10,500 spindles of self-acting mules, with spoolers and warpers, more than ten years.

By means of light belts and shafts, with high velocities, the use of the ponderous old shafting and massy cog wheels, formerly employed, has been here dispensed with. Not a single cog wheel is retained, to require replacing for broken tooth, excepting only in the wet positions of the gearing of the wheel pits, there necessary to increase the speed to the desired velocity.

These suggestions for improving and economizing the transmission of the greatest extent of motive power in mills,

18

with the least cost of materials, may be found practically useful to engineers as hints for further improvements.

Among the old papers and accounts of this mill was found the following amusing letter from one of the first superintendents, at the commencement of the business of manufacturing cotton. His pathetic account of his troubles in managing 1,000 spindles, in the olden time, may excite a smile in managers of the great cotton manufactories of the present day :

To ⸺ ⸺, *Agt., Providence.*

We spun 14,560 skeins last week; but who can count the yarn spun this week? "Why?" you will probably say; because some of it is reeled, some twisted into mule banding, and a large quantity held in reserve on bobbins. Presuming you will probably say that we ought to do as our neighbor manufacturer, P. Allen, has done, and weigh the bobbins and yarn, and then subtract the weight of the bobbins. My dear sir, we have no scales suitable to do this. Then you will say, "Why did you not send for them?" Dear sir, it is for the want of foresight and knowledge in our business. If you will send to me a suitable scale-beam of good length, say $2\frac{1}{2}$ feet long, we will try to keep some account of yarn spun. Yet, however, it is a confused mess, and wants some of your information on the subject. There are so many things to hear, see, settle, transact, digest, add, take off, increase and command,—all in and through the cotton dust, that I can hardly tell what thing ought to come first.

The dressing machine begins to rattle and blough; the looms begin to thump; and, the next you will say, "I wonder what will come next?"

Your servant wishes to know!

⸺ ⸺.

P. S.—Wanted—Codfish.
         Ginger.
         Pearl ash.
         Indian and Rye Meal.

UNION VILLAGE.

At the time that the territory of Smithfield was occupied by the Indians it was by them called Wionkheige in its

southerly section; Louisquisset in that portion round about
Lime Rock, and Woonsocket in the northerly part of the
territory. The present Union Village was originally called
Woonsocket, the name being changed when the Union Bank
was established there. The first house was built by James
Arnold, which was erected in 1690, a part of which is now
standing, an addition having been built by Judge Peleg
Arnold in 1780. Judge Arnold kept tavern here for many
years. The second house was built by Hezekiah Comstock,
in 1702, on the site where now stands the house of the late
Walter Allen, now known as the Osborne house. The Uriah
Arnold house was built by Captain Daniel Arnold in 1714.
The Friends' Meeting House was built in 1719, and was
originally 20 feet square. It was enlarged by another, as
an addition, in 1755, 20x30 feet, this addition being an ell.
In 1775 this ell was removed and an addition, 32x32 feet,
was added. In 1849 the entire building was remodeled, and
remains in the form then given it. This house stands a little
outside, and to the south of the village on the old Providence
and Worcester road. Soon after the last reconstruction the
meeting house was furnished with green blinds by Edward
Harris, Welcome Farnum and Joseph Almy. For many
years this was the only public house of worship in this
vicinity, and as there were many Friends resident in the
surrounding country it was usually filled on " First Day "
with an intelligent and devout congregation.

The Friends moved at an early date in behalf of education. In 1771 they declared that " It is thought necessary
that poor children be schooled," and Moses Farnum, Moses
Brown, Thomas Lapham, Job Scott, Elisha Thornton, Samuel
Aldrich, George Arnold, Antepast Earle and David Steere
were appointed to draw up a plan establishing a free school
among Friends. Report having been made recommending
the organizing of said free schools, and Thomas Steere,
Moses Farnum, David Steere, Moses Brown, Ezekiel Com-

stock, Benjamin Arnold, Rufus Smith, Daniel Cross, George Smith, Samuel Aldrich, Gardner Earle, David Buffum and Thomas Lapham, Jr., were appointed to select the places for the schools, to inspect the poorer sort of Friends' families, to determine who shall be schooled from the fund, and generally to transact all other matters and things belonging to the school.

In 1718 " Providence monthly meeting" was set off from "Greenwich monthly meeting," and consisted of Providence and Mendon meetings. The name was changed, in 1731, to " Smithfield monthly meeting." In 1783 the present Providence monthly meeting was set off from Smithfield monthly meeting.

The Smithfield Academy, located at Union Village, was for a long time a flourishing and useful institution. It was built by lottery, and was occupied in 1810. David Aldrich was the first teacher, who was succeded by Josiah Clark. John Thornton, who came next on the list, remained for about six years, when he was followed by George D. Prentice, afterwards so well known as the editor of the Louisville (Ky.) *Journal.* Other teachers were employed, among them Christopher Robinson, who thereafter became a prominent lawyer, residing in the present village of Woonsocket, and who has been Attorney General of the State, member of the House of Representatives of the United States, and United States Minister to Peru. The last teacher was James Bushee, who taught almost continuously for twenty years, impressing upon the school a character for solidity and effectiveness. When, about the year 1850, he closed his connection with the Academy, not only did it cease to exist, but the last effort to induce or retain business or material life in this attractive village expired.

About half a mile north of the village is one of those natural curiosities occasionally found, of interest to the idlest observer, as well as to the geologist. "Coblin Rock" is of uniform diameter, standing on a large flat rock, and weighs probably about 200 tons. Near this were situated the quarries from which the once famous "Smithfield Scythe Stones" were taken. It is estimated that not less than 500,000 dozen of these stones were made, during a period of about twenty years. The makers were, at different times, Marcus Arnold, George Aldrich, Thomas A. Paine and Hanson Arnold.

To the southwest, and at a short distance from Union Village, is situated Woonsocket Hill, the highest land in the State of Rhode Island. Its summit is 570 feet above high-water mark at Providence; it is composed mostly of granular quartz, mica, and tulc. On the highest part of this hill is a large pond.

For the last forty years there has been no increase in the number of dwelling houses in Union Village; two have been removed, and two erected, and yet there is (1870) no land for sale. The population is 125, and the picturesqueness and quiet of this ancient village are equalled by the intelligence, conservatism and virtues of its inhabitants.

THE VALLEY OF THE MOSHASSUCK.

The valley of the Moshassuck, along which the early settlers of Providence pushed northward almost from the first, was originally a region of great natural beauty, and has been the locality wherein the most successful business enterprises have alternated with the most disastrous experiments. The "Lime Rock" country is diversified by hills, possesses a soil rich and permanent, and has been, for more than the life of the town, the centre of the manufacture of lime of the very highest quality. While this territory was yet a part of the town of Providence it was provided by law that the limestone quarries should be and remain the property of the town; they were not to be set off as other lands, to the inhabitants, nor sold. This attempt at sovereign prerogative failed, however, although the town of Smithfield made some inef fectual attempts to revive it. The result was that the invaluable quarries went into private hands.

The manufacture of lime has been carried on with great success, and continuously, by the Dexter Lime Rock Company, and the Harris Lime Rock Company, and their predecessors. The village of Lime Rock, which at one time was the location of the Lime Rock Bank, and the seat of considerable local business, is now, owing to the construction of the Providence and Worcester Railroad, and the tendency of the times toward centralization of capital, indeed a " deserted village."

Passing down the valley one reaches within a few miles the Quinsnicket country, Quinsnicket signifying in the Indian language " the large place of rock houses." So recently as in the days of the late Stephen H. Smith the ruins of many of the Indian huts were in existence upon his place. Mr. Smith, who was an admirer of nature, a most advanced and excellent horticulturist and an indefatigable improver of whatever locality he had possession of, beautified the immediate vicinity of his residence, at Quinsnicket, by damming the Moshassuck and forming a beautiful lake, and by surrounding his house with such a wealth of trees, plants and creeping vines as to make it one of the most noticeable situations of the town.

The " Butterfly Factory," located in the immediate vicinity of the house of Mr. Smith, was originally erected for a cotton mill. It has been used for various purposes, but never with any permanent commercial success. Just below this building is a small privilege which was first occupied by Samuel Arnold, who, about the year 1816, established a distillery there. This enterprise proving unremunerative, Mr. Arnold and the late ex-Governor Lemuel H. Arnold, about 1826, converted the establishment into a print works, under the name of the Arnoldville Printing Company. This company was soon dissolved, and Holder C. Weeden took the place of ex-Governor Arnold. The concern was, not long after, burnt to the ground. It was rebuilt, Mr. Weeden carrying on the business, but was again, about 1844, destroyed by fire. In 1846 Theodore Schroeder took possession of the establishment, which had been rebuilt, and changed the name to "Manchester Printworks," and for a time was eminently successful, but it was blown up by the explosion of steam boilers, and Mr. Schroeder failed about the year 1858. The works were again rebuilt and operated by Brown, Dean & Macready, who failed about 1862. The establishment having been purchased by Messrs. W. F. & F. C. Sayles, was occupied by the American Worsted Co., for the manufacture of worsted braids and yarns. This was the first attempt to manufacture worsted braids in this country, and the poineer in a business which has since been developed to such an extent as to supply the needs of the country and practically shut out imported braid. The company consisted of Messrs. W. F. & F. C. Sayles, Darius Goff and D. L. Goff. In 1864 the company was dissolved, the Messrs. Goff starting the business at Pawtucket, and Messrs. W. F. & F. C. Sayles continued the old business under the name of the Union Worsted Co., until 1867, when the buildings and machinery were burned to the ground. This was the end, so far, of the attempt to manufacture on this site.

The Friends' Meeting House, situated just below the last mentioned privilege, was erected prior to 1708. On October 2, 1708, Eleazer Arnold deeded to Thomas Smith and others a tract of land near the dwelling house of said Eleazer Arnold, seven rods by twelve, "on which stands a certain meeting house, of the people called Quakers." This has been known for many years as "Lower Smithfield meeting house." It still stands in a good state of preservation, and is occupied, although not with the same regularity, nor by the same full congregations as in days of yore.

A little further down stream will be seen the Moshassuck Bleachery, owned by W. F. & F. C. Sayles. This establishment was commenced in 1848, has increased in extent and facilities without interruption, and rapidly, and is without doubt the most extensive and completely equipped bleachery in the country, as it has been one of the most profitable. Not only are the buildings requisite for the business of the most substantial character, but the dwellings erected for the operatives are neat and commodious, while not a few of the employés own their residences and land sufficient to give opportunity for the display of agricultural taste. Beyond this the whole tone of the vicinage is healthy. The proprietors not only encourage, but pecuniarily aid every effort in behalf of temperance, of education, and of religious welfare. Here, where a quarter of a century ago there was nothing but the wilderness or a sandy waste, is now a thrifty, an attractive, a prosperous and exemplary village, destined to become still more conspicuous and progressive.

DIVISION OF THE TOWN.

There had been for several years a feeling on the part of many of the inhabitants of the town, that it should be divided. Various attempts had been made to set a portion off to Woonsocket, and the aid of the General Assembly had been invoked to favor such a project, but it was opposed by the Representatives and Senator from the town, acting under instructions from the tax-payers, and was defeated. The matter, however, was not allowed to drop, and on Saturday, January 21, 1871, a special meeting of the freemen was called at the Town House. After a full and free discussion, the question "shall the town be divided?" was carried in the affirmative by a vote of 111 to 33.

The following resolution was then adopted without a dissenting vote:—

"*Resolved*, That this meeting favors a division of the town of Smithfield, according to the act now on the Moderator's table, making the new towns of North Smithfield and Greenville."

Afterwards the act was amended so as to leave the old name Smithfield to that portion of the town designated in the act as Greenville, giving the name of Lincoln to that portion which had been designed to be left as Smithfield. The following is the act as finally adopted:

AN ACT SETTING OFF A PORTION OF SMITHFIELD TO WOONSOCKET, AND DIVIDING THE REMAINDER INTO THREE TOWNS.

Passed March 8, 1871.

It is enacted by the General Assembly as follows:

SECTION 1. All that portion of the town of Smithfield lying and being within the following boundaries, that is to say, beginning at a point on the southerly line of said town of Smithfield, where the Douglas Pike (so-called) crosses said line in or over the Wenscott Reservoir; thence running easterly with and on said town line to the centre of the Blackstone River, being the southeasterly corner of said town of Smithfield; thence running with the centre of said Blackstone River, being the easterly boundary of said town to a point in the centre of said river, opposite the centre of the mouth of the Crook Fall River; thence running by and with the centre of said Crook Fall River to a point where the road leading from the Providence and Worcester road (so-called) past the house of Ephraim Sayles crosses the said Crook Fall River; thence running southerly on a straight line to the place of beginning, is hereby incorporated into a township by the name of Lincoln; and the inhabitants thereof shall have and enjoy the like benefits, liberties, privileges and immunities, and be subject to like duties and responsibilities, as the other towns in this State generally enjoy and are subject to.

SEC. 2. All persons liable to pay taxes in said town of Lincoln shall be holden to pay to the collectors of the town of Smithfield all arrears of taxes legally assessed on them in said Smithfield before the passage of this act.

SEC. 3. The said town of Lincoln shall and may send to the Gen-

19

eral Assembly two representatives, until the next reapportionment of representatives by the General Assembly.

SEC. 4.   There shall be drawn in the town of Lincoln for the Supreme Court, when holden in the county of Providence, and for the Court of Common Pleas in said county, one grand and four petit jurors.

SEC. 5.   The said town of Lincoln, for the purposes of representation in the General Assembly of this State, shall be considered a town on and after the first Wednesday in April next; and shall be considered a town for all purposes whatsoever, on and after the first Monday in June next.

SEC. 6.   The trial justice in the third voting district in the town of Smithfield, as at present organized, is hereby empowered to issue his warrant to any officer or other person whom he may appoint, to warn the qualified voters of the town of Lincoln to meet for the purposes required by law and the provisions of this act, on the first Wednesday in April next; on the first Monday in June next, and on the second Tuesday in June next.

SEC. 7.   The annual election of town clerk, council, treasurer and justices of the peace for said town of Lincoln, shall be held on the first Monday in June.   The annual town meeting for the purpose of ordering a town tax, school and highway tax, and for the transaction of such other business as may legally come before said meeting shall be held on the second Tuesday in June.

SEC. 8.   The town council of said town of Lincoln shall, at their first meeting next after their annual election, choose and elect so many town officers as by the laws of the State are or shall be required, excepting such as by this act are directed to be otherwise elected.

SEC. 9.   The town council of said town of Lincoln elected as herein provided shall, at some meeting previous to the annual election, determine the number of justices of the peace to be elected by the people.   Whenever any vacancy occurs in any of the officers of or in said town of Lincoln that are filled by the electors of said town at the annual election, the town council shall order a new election, and such election shall be notified and conducted according to law and the provisions herein contained.

SEC. 10.   The town council of the town of Smithfield shall make out a correct alphabetical list of all persons resident in said town of Lincoln entitled to vote in said town under article second, section first, of the constitution of this State, and a list of all persons entitled to vote by registry, and the payment of registry and other taxes, or by the performance of military duty; and shall cause the said list to be

certified and delivered to the trial justice in and for the third voting
district in said Smithfield, to be by him delivered to the moderator
who shall preside at the first meeting of the electors of the said town
of Lincoln. Said council shall also cause a corrected list of all persons
entitled to vote as aforesaid, to be certified and delivered to the said
justice, to be by him delivered to the moderator who shall preside at
the meeting of said electors on the first Monday in June next.

SEC. 11. All that part of the town of Smithfield lying and being
within the following limits, to wit: beginning at a point on the State
line between the States of Rhode Island and Massachusetts, being the
point where the towns of Uxbridge, in Massachusetts, and Smithfield
and Burrillville, in Rhode Island, meet, and are bounded, it being the
northwest corner of the town of Smithfield; thence running southerly,
on and with the west line of said town of Smithfield to a point being
the northeast corner of the town of Glocester, where the northerly
line of said Glocester and the southerly line of the town of Burrillville
meet the westerly line of said Smithfield; thence running easterly to
a point where the road leading from the Providence and Worcester
road, (so-called,) by the house of Ephraim Sayles, crosses the Crook
Fall River, near the house of Simon Newell; thence with said Crook
Fall River, and the centre thereof, to a point being the centre of the
mouth of said Crook Fall River, and the centre of the Blackstone
River; thence in a straight line westerly to a point on the southerly
line of the Providence and Worcester road, (so-called,) at the Booth
pond, (so-called); thence with the southerly line of said road, exclud-
ing said road, to a point on the same, where the road leading from
Woonsocket Falls village to the Union village enters said road a little
northerly of the Friends' meeting house; thence northerly in a straight
line towards the easterly corner of the covered bridge, near the Blackstone Manufacturing Company's mill, until a point is reached due
west from the centre of the dam of an ancient grist mill; thence
running due east to the centre of Blackstone River; thence running
with said river on the present town line of Smithfield, to the State
line, it being the northeast corner of the town of Smithfield; thence
running westerly on and with the northerly line of said town of Smithfield to the place of beginning, is hereby set off and incorporated into
the township by the name of Slater; and the inhabitants thereof shall
have and enjoy the like benefits, privileges and immunities, and be
subject to like duties and responsibilities as the other towns in this
State generally enjoy and are subject to.

SEC. 12. All persons liable to pay taxes in said town of Slater shall
be holden to pay to the collectors of the town of Smithfield all arrears

of taxes legally assessed on them, in said Smithfield, before the passage of this act.

Sec. 13.   The said town of Slater may, and shall send to the General Assembly two representatives, until the next reapportionment of representatives by the State.

Sec. 14.   There shall be drawn in the town of Slater, for the Supreme Court, when holden in the county of Providence, and for the Court of Common Pleas, in said county, one grand and two petit jurors.

Sec. 15.   The said town of Slater, for the purposes of representation in the General Assembly of this State, shall be considered a town on and after the first Wednesday in April next; and shall be considered a town for all purposes whatsoever, on and after the first Monday in June next.

Sec. 16.   William H. Seagrave is hereby empowered to issue his warrant to any officer or other person whom he may appoint to warn the qualified electors of the town of Slater, to meet for the purposes required by law and the provisions of this act, on the first Wednesday in April next, and on the first Monday in June next.

Sec. 17.   The annual election of town clerk, town council, treasurer, and justices of the peace, for said town of Slater, shall be held on the first Monday in June, and for the transaction of other town business, which may properly be presented, shall be held on the second Monday in June.

Sec. 18.   The town council of said town of Slater shall, at its first meeting next after the annual election of such town council, choose and elect so many town officers as by the laws of the State are, or shall be required, excepting such as are by this act directed to be otherwise elected.

Sec. 19.   The town council of said town of Slater, elected as herein provided, shall, at some meeting previous to the annual election, determine the number of justices of the peace to be elected by the people.   Whenever any vacancy occurs in any of the offices of said town of Slater, that are filled by the electors of said town, at the annual election, the town council shall order a new election, and such election shall be notified and conducted according to law and the provisions herein contained.

Sec. 20.   The town council of the town of Smithfield shall make out a correct alphabetical list of all persons resident in said town of Slater, entitled to vote in said town, under article second, section first, of the constitution of this State, and a list of all persons entitled to vote by registry, and the payment of registry or other taxes, or by the performance of military duty; and shall cause the said list to be certified and delivered to said William H. Seagrave, to be by him delivered to the moderator who shall preside at the first meeting of the electors of the said town of Slater. Said council shall also cause a corrected list of all persons entitled to vote as aforesaid, to be certified and delivered to the said Seagrave, to be by him delivered to the moderator who shall preside at the meeting of said electors, on the first Monday of June next.

SEC. 21. The town of Lincoln shall be liable for the support of all persons who now do, or who shall hereafter, stand in need of relief as paupers, whose settlement was gained by or derived from a settlement within the limits of said town of Lincoln, as described by this act. And the town of Slater shall be in like case or cases equally liable for the support of persons needing relief as paupers, whose settlement was gained by or derived from a settlement within its limits, as described by this act.

SEC. 22. The indebtedness of the town of Smithfield, as at present defined, shall be apportioned between and paid by the towns of Lincoln, Smithfield and Slater, as organized by this act, and the territory herein set off and annexed to the town of Woonsocket, in proportion to the ratable property in said towns and territory, according to the last assessment in and by the town of Smithfield, as at present organized. The town of Slater shall be, and is hereby empowered to assess upon the persons and estates in the territory hereby set off and annexed, and collect the ratable proportion of the debt of the town of Smithfield, which said annexed territory would be liable to pay if it had remained as a part of the town of Slater, and the money arising therefrom shall pay over as a part of the sum provided for the payment of the indebtedness of said town of Smithfield; and in case said town and territory aforesaid shall not agree in respect to the division, apportionment and payment of said indebtedness, the Court of Common Pleas for the county of Providence shall, upon the petition of either town, appoint three competent and disinterested persons to hear the parties and make award therein; and their award, or that of any two of them, accepted by the court aforesaid, shall be final.

SEC. 23. The books of records and papers of the town of Smithfield shall be and remain in the custody of the town of Lincoln, but the inhabitants of the town of Smithfield, and of the town of Slater, shall at all times have access to the same, in like manner, and under like conditions as if the town of Smithfield had not been divided. The town clerk of the town of Smithfield shall, as soon as may be, after the passage of this act, cause so much of the said records as relates to lands in the town of Smithfield, as the same shall be bounded, after the passage of this act; and so much as relates to lands in the town of Slater, as have been made since the year 1850, to be transcribed and copied for the use of the said towns respectively, the expense thereof to be charged to the said town of Smithfield, as at present organized. And such transcripts or copies shall have all and the same validity as the original record.

SEC. 24. Said towns of Smithfield and Slater shall provide books for the registry of land titles, and such other records as are and may be required by the laws of this State, to be kept by the several towns therein.

SEC. 25. The town and other officers shall continue to exercise their several offices in the towns of Smithfield and Slater, so far as pertains to town affairs, until the election of officers in the towns of Lincoln and Slater, and until their successors be qualified to act.

SEC. 26. The school commissioner shall apportion the school money in the towns of Lincoln, Smithfield and Slater, in accordance with the last census taken by the authority of the United States in the town of Smithfield, and published, to be divided as follows: The school committee of the town of Smithfield shall cause the census to be taken prior to the first day of June next, in the towns of Smithfield and Slater, of all children under fifteen years of age, and report the number of said children in each town to the said commissioner; and he shall distribute the school money to each town in ratio to the number of children in each town, to the apportionment made to the towns of Lincoln, Smithfield and Slater under the last census, under which apportionment has been made.

SEC. 27. The town councils of the said towns of Lincoln and Slater may each remove all officers by them respectively appointed, for misconduct or incapacity, at any regular meeting of said councils.

SEC. 28. All that portion of the town of Smithfield lying northerly and easterly of a line commencing at a point in the centre of the Blackstone River, directly opposite the mouth of Crook Fall River; thence running northwesterly in a direct line to the southerly line, and including it, of the Providence and Worcester road, (so-called,) at the Booth pond, (so-called); thence running on and with the southerly line of said Providence and Worcester road, and including said road, to a point where the road leading from Woonsocket Falls village to the Union village enters said Providence and Worcester road near the Friends' meeting house; thence in a direct line northerly towards the easterly corner of the covered bridge, near the Blackstone Manufacturing Company's mill, until the line reaches a point due west from the centre of the dam, by what was an ancient grist mill; thence running due east to the centre of the Blackstone River, is hereby set off from said town of Smithfield, and annexed to the town of Woonsocket, and the portion so set off and annexed is hereby declared to be within the limits and jurisdiction of said town of Woonsocket, for all purposes except as herein provided; and the inhabitants of the said portion so set off and annexed shall have and enjoy all the rights, privileges and immunities, and be subject to all the duties and liabilities which the inhabitants of said town of Woonsocket have and enjoy, and to which they are subject.

SEC. 29. The town of Woonsocket shall be liable for the support of all persons who now do, or who shall hereafter stand in need of relief as paupers, whose settlement was gained by or derived from a settlement within the limits of the portion of the said town of Smithfield hereby set off and annexed.

SEC. 30. All persons and estates in said portion of said town of Smithfield so annexed shall be holden to pay to the town of Smithfield all arrears of taxes legally assessed therein prior to the passage of this act, in the same manner as if this act had not been passed.

SEC. 31. All the books of records of said town of Smithfield shall be the property and remain in the custody of the town of Lincoln, incorporated by this act; but the inhabitants of the portion of Smithfield set off and annexed as aforesaid shall have the same right of access to the same as if this act had not been passed; and the town clerk of the town of Smithfield shall, as soon as may be after the passage of this act, cause so much of said records as relates to land in said portion so set off and annexed as have been made since the year 1850, to be transcribed and copied for the use of said town of Woonsocket, the expense whereof shall be paid by said town of Woonsocket; and said transcripts and copies shall be deposited in the office of the town clerk, in said town of Woonsocket, and certified copies thereof shall have the same validity as certified copies from the original record.

SEC. 32. The school commissioner shall apportion the school money for said town of Smithfield, and the portion of said town hereby set off and annexed, as aforesaid, in accordance with the last census taken by the authority of the United States, in the said town of Smithfield, under which an apportionment has been made, to be divided as follows: The school committee of the said town of Smithfield shall cause a census to be taken prior to the first day of June, A. D. 1871, of all the children under the age of fifteen years in said Smithfield, and in the portion of said town hereby set off and annexed, and shall report the same to said school commissioner, and he shall

distribute said school money to said town of Smithfield, as hereinbe-
fore provided, and to the said town of Woonsocket, in ratio to the
number of children in said town of Smithfield as at present organized,
exclusive of the portion hereby set off and annexed, and in said portion
so set off and annexed to the apportionment made to the town of
Smithfield under the last census under which an apportionment has
been made, until the publication of the census taken under the
authority of the United States, in the year A. D. 1870. The towns
of Smithfield and Woonsocket shall pay in equal proportions the expense of taking said census.

SEC. 33. The said town of Smithfield shall assume and remain
holden for all debts and other liabilities of said town, arising out of
any contract made by said town prior to the passage of this act; and
for all claims hereafter arising in consequence of anything done, or
omitted to be done by said town, prior to the passage of this act; and
the town of Woonsocket, as at present constituted, shall pay to the
town of Smithfield, as at present constituted, on or before the first
day of May, A. D. 1871, the sum of seven thousand five hundred
dollars.

SEC. 34. Except as provided in section 33, of this act, all rights
and remedies of every kind or nature, which said town of Smithfield
had or was entitled to, in any wise growing out of or pertaining to
that portion of said town, set off and annexed as aforesaid, shall be-
long and appertain to said town of Woonsocket, and except as provided in said section 33, all the obligations, duties and liabilities
which said town of Smithfield is now under or in any way subject to,
rising out of, or pertaining to the portion set off or annexed, are
hereby imposed upon, and shall be assumed by the town of Woonsocket, in the same manner and to the same extent as said town of
Smithfield would have been liable therefor if this act had not been
passed; and all suits and proceedings in relation thereto shall be
brought by and against said town of Woonsocket.

SEC. 35. All proceedings, civil and criminal, commenced or pending prior to the passage of this act, before the trial justice in said
portion set off and annexed as aforesaid, shall remain within the
jurisdiction of said justice, who is hereby authorized to proceed to
final judgment and execution therein, as if this act had not been
passed.

SEC. 36. All proceedings commenced or pending, prior to the
passage of this act, before the Court of Probate of the town of Smithfield, arising from or within said portion set off and annexed as aforesaid, shall remain within the jurisdiction of said Court of Probate of

the town of Smithfield, which said court is hereby authorized to proceed upon said matters, as if this act had not been passed.

SEC. 37. Except as provided in sections 35 and 36, of this act, the town and other officers of the town elected by said town of Smithfield shall continue to exercise their several offices in said portion set off and annexed as aforesaid, so far as relates to town business, until the next annual election in the town of Woonsocket, and until the officers elected at such election shall be qualified to act.

SEC. 38. The court of magistrates of Woonsocket shall, from and after the passage of this act, have exclusive jurisdiction (except as provided in section 35, of this act,) within the limits of said portion set off and annexed as aforesaid, in all civil actions and criminal cases and proceedings whatsoever, jurisdiction over which is, or may have been given by law to the trial justice residing in said portion set off and annexed as aforesaid.

SEC. 39. From and after the passage of this act the valuation of the town of Smithfield as it then remains, as a basis of the State tax provided by Chapter 749 of the Statutes, shall be $1,762,443; and the valuation of Woonsocket, for the purpose aforesaid, shall be $6,208,-632; the valuation of the town of Lincoln, for the purpose aforesaid, shall be $4,406,107; and the valuation of the town of Slater, for the purpose aforesaid, shall be $1,762,443.

SEC. 40. The town clerk of said town of Smithfield shall, on or before the fourth day of April, A. D. 1871, transmit to the town clerk of said town of Woonsocket a certified list of all persons residing in said portion set off and annexed as aforesaid, who would have been qualified to vote in said Smithfield on the fifth day of April, A. D. 1871, upon any proposition to impose a tax on or for the expenditure of money in said Smithfield had this act not been passed. And also a certified list of all persons residing therein, who might have been qualified to vote for general officers on said fifth day of April, A. D. 1871, had not this act been passed.

SEC. 41. The town farm, town house, furniture, stock and tools now the property of the town of Smithfield shall be and remain the property of the town of Smithfield, as the same should be bounded after the passage of this act.

SEC. 42. On or before the second Monday in June next the town of Smithfield, as at present organized, shall pay to the town of Slater, incorporated by this act, the sum of five thousand dollars; and on or before the second day of June next shall pay to the town of Lincoln, incorporated by this act, the sum of two thousand five hundred dollars.

20

SEC. 43.   The bridewell in the village of Bernon, the property of the town of Smithfield, shall be and remain the property of the town of Woonsocket.

SEC. 44.   The poor in the asylum of the town of Smithfield shall be taken care of by the town of Smithfield until the towns of Lincoln and Slater shall respectively have reasonable time to provide for such as they may be legally liable to take charge of, said town of Smithfield to be paid the actual amount expended in keeping said paupers.

SEC. 45.   Charles Moics, Job Shaw, Arlon Mowry and Cyrus Arnold are hereby appointed a committee to run the lines and set up stone bounds between the several towns named in this act, and to apportion equitably the expense thereof between said towns, which said towns shall be held to pay.

SEC. 46.   Charles Moies, Latimer W. Ballou and Bradbury C. Hill, are hereby appointed a committee to adjust equitably the proportion of any of the debt of the town of Woonsocket, which the portion hereby set off, and annexed of and from Smithfield, should assume and pay, and their report, or that of any two of them, shall be final.

SEC. 47.   All appropriations made by the town of Smithfield prior to the passage of this act, shall be paid and expended in the same manner, and upon and for the same territory as though this act had not been passed.

SEC. 48.   The town of Smithfield as bounded and organized after the passage of this act, may and shall send to the General Assembly one representative until the next re-apportionment of representatives by the State.

SEC. 49.   There shall be drawn in the town of Smithfield as constituted after the passage of this act, for the supreme court, when holden in the county of Providence, and for the court of common pleas, in said county, one grand and two petit jurors.

SEC. 50.   The town of Lincoln shall be divided into two voting districts.   Voting district number one shall comprise all the territory in said town, which is now voting district number three, in the present town of Smithfield.   Voting district number two shall consist of all the remaining territory in said town of Lincoln.

SEC. 51.   All business commenced, or pending before the court of probate of the town of Smithfield, as at present organized, which shall be and remain unfinished on the second Tuesday of June next, shall be transferred to, and proceeded with and concluded by the town council of the town of Lincoln, in like manner, and with the same effect as the same would and might have been proceeded with, and concluded by the court of probate of Smithfield, if this act had not been passed, and the records thereof shall be made and kept in the books of the town of Smithfield, as at present organized.

SEC. 52. The town of Woonsocket as constituted by this act, may and shall send to the General Assembly three representatives until the next reäpportionment of representatives by the State.

SEC. 53. All acts and parts of acts inconsistent herewith, are hereby repealed.

AN ACT IN ADDITION TO AND IN AMENDMENT OF AN ACT (PASSED AT THE PRESENT JANUARY SESSION) SETTING OFF A PORTION OF SMITHFIELD TO WOONSOCKET, AND DIVIDING THE REMAINDER INTO THREE TOWNS.

Passed March 24, 1871.

It is enacted by the General Assembly as follows :

SECTION 1. Section eleven of said act is hereby amended by changing the name of Slater in said section, to that of North Smithfield; also, in each subsequent section, where the name of Slater appears, it is hereby changed to that of North Smithfield.

SEC. 2. William H. Seagraves is hereby empowered to issue his warrant to any officer or other person whom he may appoint to warn the qualified electors of the town of North Smithfield to meet for the purposes required by law and the provisions of this act on the second Monday in June, 1871.

SEC. 3. So much of the act to which this is in amendment as requires either of the towns named therein, to draw Grand jurors for the Supreme Court for the county of Providence is hereby repealed.

SEC. 4. All acts and parts of acts inconsistent herewith are hereby repealed.

SEC. 5. This act shall take effect from and after its passage.

Smithfield was the largest town in the State ; it was incorporated, (being set off from Providence,) in 1730, and was always an important municipality. It is not strange that many of her citizens regretted the change of circumstances which demanded her dismemberment, although almost all had come to see that the thing was inevitable, and the vast majority to feel that, sentiment aside, a division would be preferable in all respects. Woonsocket gains something like three thousand in population, and two millions of taxable property, making its population, speaking roundly, twelve thousand, and its valuation six millions of dollars. Never in its history was this thriving place in a more promising condition. In addition to the large woolen and cotton mills which have so long stood as monuments of its enterprise, and many of which have recently been much enlarged, it now proposes a large establishment for the manufacture of rubber goods, a washing and wringing machine factory, a large foundry, with other and different manufactures, giving it a varied and prosperous industry. The returns of the six institutions for savings, which are located here, show a very gratifying condition, pecuniarily speaking, of the inhabitants. There is accumulated capital, every facility, save tide water, for doing business, real estate is advancing, manufacturers, merchants and business men generally are on a firm and substantial foundation, and Woonsocket is growing rapidly and safely. With its now diversified and important interests, its easy and rapid communication with Providence, Boston and New York, its mechanical ingenuity and appliances, its pure water and healthy location, it is destined, humanly speaking, to become one of the most active and populous, as well as wealthy towns in the State.

The town of Slater, being the northernmost of the towns carved out of old Smithfield, comprises about twenty-five square miles, and its valuation, in the act of division, 1,762,-443 dollars. Within its limits is that portion of the Waterford woolen mills which lie in Rhode Island, a valuable but unimproved water power at Branch village, the scythe works of Mansfield Lamb at Forestdale, the Forestdale cotton mills, the village of Slatersville with its busy mills and thousands of spindles, and the beautiful Union Village, which, although deserted by trade, was a lively place before Woonsocket, known save for its falls, its grist mill, and pine hills, and is still, in some respects one of the most attractive locations in this vicinity. This town may be as economically managed as any town need be. The two important bridges, one of wood at the Branch Village, and the stone arched bridge at Slatersville, are in good condition, and the latter will need no repairs, apparently, for a century to come. The farmers are, as a rule, well-to-do; school-houses are sufficiently numerous and large, the roads are in good order, and without littleness, the population is prudent, and conservative, without being indifferent to a genuine progress. Largely agricultural, the farmers find their markets in the adjoining villages, and fully appreciate the fact that without these villages their lands would be of comparatively little value. Their wood, their butter, their poultry and vegetables bring good prices and ready sale, and it is easy to see that a compact town, where every man knows every other man, and meets him often, will be more carefully, not to say honestly managed and governed than one twenty miles in length with many conflicting and sectional interests, the population of which rarely ever comes together except once a year at the June town meeting, to protect or plunder, as the case may be, the town treasury. Seventeen thousand people, scattered over seventy-five square miles, part living in compact villages, and part in the rural districts, can scarcely be said to be a homogeneous, and experience has shown, is not likely to be an harmonious population.

The town of Smithfield, as at present bounded, lies south of Slater and west of the new town of Lincoln. It covers an area of twenty-eight square miles, is very nearly a square in form, and is rated in the act of division, at the same valuation as the town of Slater. Within its limits are the manufacturing villages of Georgiaville, Allendale and Greenville, the latter the largest, and a very pretty village. This town has the smallest population of the three, into which the old town has been divided. It has more roads in proportion to its population and wealth than either of the others, although its bridges are less expensive. It retains the old town house and town farm, as well as the name, to which its inhabitants clung with great and very proper pertinacity, inasmuch as it is likely to remain intact, and to preserve the old traditions and habits longer than would either of the others. More repugnance was felt in regard to the division, in this section of old Smithfield than elsewhere; for a long time the feeling against it was almost universal, and it was only the logic of events, which, and as they thought rather expensively, influenced the people of this region to acquiesce in the new order of things. In the arrangement of representatives, new Smithfield took only one, although she has not for many years been honored with the Senator. She will hereafter have a member in the upper house, and is quite capable of sending one worthy to sit in, and aid the deliberations of that body. Greenville will be the central and prominent village in this town, and with the renewal of operations in the large woolen mills there, we shall hope to see it enter upon a new era of prosperity. One thing is certain, this will be a substantial town, which will, in all that goes toward making a vigorous and progressive community, be an honor and an advantage to the State.

Lincoln lies south of Woonsocket and east of Smithfield. It contains about eighteen square miles, and has a valuation of 4,406,107 dollars. In this town are Manville, Albion, Ashton, Lonsdale, Valley Falls and Central Falls. The population is about nine thousand. This it will be seen is the smallest and wealthiest of the three towns. Bounded on the east by the Blackstone river, with great manufacturing interests, with the compact and go-a-head village of Central Falls, it will be as busy and as productive as almost any town in the State. In the nature of things, however, it is not likely to remain as at present limited for any great length of time. At Manville, the mills are in Cumberland, while the village is in Lincoln; at Ashton the mill and one village are in Cumberland, while another village belonging to the same company is in Lincoln; at Albion, the case is the same as at

Manville; at Lonsdale, the Lonsdale Company have on the one side of the river in Lincoln, a large establishment, comprising several mills and a bleachery, and over the river, in Cumberland, a large mill and its accompanying village. Valley Falls is situated—mills and village on both sides of the river, and Central Falls is in like condition, and spreading rapidly on either side. If there was any reason—and there were cogent and conclusive reasons—for what has now been done, a short time will probable suffice to show that much more is to be done to meet the necessities of the times, and keep pace with the requirements of our ever increasing industries, and the progress of the people in pecuniary, social and governmental affairs. In many respects Central Falls is a model of enterprise, and it has perhaps, within its limits as many different branches of business as any place of its size anywhere. Should it hereafter be joined to Pawtucket, Pawtucket would be certainly industriously managed, and without doubt, judiciously and profitably. But we were to write only of what is, not of what is to be, or may be.

The Smithfield which Samuel F. Man, Lewis Dexter, Sessions Mowry, Asa Winsor, Thomas Mann, Thomas Buffum, Joseph Wilkinson and Morton Mowry knew, is a thing of the past. They and others as able and original though less known, made an impress upon it which lasts and is a force even yet. The ancient town house has resounded with their quaint and sensible remarks, the town council is yet imbued with many of their ideas; and so strong were their intellects and so powerful their wills, that even the great change in the business, wants and population in the town, has not sufficed to efface their influence.

But we have no right to live wholly in the past; new circumstances create new duties, and we shall best pay tribute to the memory of such men as we have named, by performing in our day and generation that which is required of us, as earnestly, and if possible, as effectually as they did in theirs.   Agriculture has given place to manufacture ; a rural population, measurably, to villages ; the stage coach is almost forgotten ; railroads, steam and the telegraph are the symbols and medium of our daily life ; our eyes are turned forward, and with an almost unconscious sigh in losing the old, we look with hope and trust to the new.   We shall not wholly forget the past, may we realize our confidence in the future,   And so, Old Smithfield, " Hail, and Farewell."

APPENDIX A.

LIST OF CITIZENS OF SMITHFIELD, WHO HAVE HELD THE
OFFICES HEREINAFTER DESIGNATED.

Members of the Continental Congress.

Peleg Arnold..1787 to 1789
Daniel Mowry...1780 to 1782

Speakers of the House of Representatives of the State of Rhode Island.

Thomas Steere .... May, 1853, to January, 1854
(Resigned, having been appointed U. S. Consul at Dundee, Scotland.)
Sullivan Ballou ....1857 to 1858.

Presidential Electors.

Stephen Stone..1844
William S. Slater...1864 to 1876

LIST OF JUSTICES OF THE SUPREME COURT AND COURT OF
COMMON PLEAS, IN AND FOR THE COUNTY OF PROV-
IDENCE, FROM SMITHFIELD.

Chief Justice of the Supreme Court.

Peleg Arnold ....May, 1796, to June 1809
Peleg Arnold............................May, 1810, to May, 1812

Assistant Justices.

Gideon Comstock.........................May, 1766, to May, 1767
Gideon Comstock ....June, 1769, to June, 1770
Gideon Comstock.......................May, 1779, to May, 1781
Thomas Buffum ....May, 1819 to May, 1823

21

Justices of the Court of Common Pleas.

Major William Jenckes, C. J .... 1734—1737
Major William Jenckes, C. J .... 1743—1745
David Comstock .... 1747—1749
Thomas Lapham .... 1750—1760
David Comstock, C. J .... 1761—1762
Thomas Lapham .... 1763—1764
David Comstock .... 1765—1768
Caleb Aldrich   ....:........... 1769—1774
Daniel Mowry, Jr .... 1776—1780
Caleb Aldrich.. .... 1781—1787
Abraham Mathewson .... 1788—1793
Arnold Paine .... 1794—1802
Thomas Mann .... 1806—1809
Thomas Mann, C. J   1810
Samuel Hill, Jr .... 1811—1817
Thomas Mann .... 1818—1820
Thomas Mann, C. J .... 1821—1832
Lewis Dexter   1835
David Daniels .... 1838—1839
George L. Barnes   1840
Lewis Dexter   1841

APPENDIX B.

1848 to 1849................................Gideon Bradford.
1850...Thomas Buffum.
1850 to 1852................................Gideon Bradford.
1853 to 1854...............................Robert Harris.
1855 to 1856.......... ....Stephen N. Mason.
1857.......................-................Daniel N. Paine.
1858 to 1859.................... ....Stephen N. Mason.
1860 to 1861.......... ....,...........William S. Slater.
1862.......................... ....Stephen N. Mason.
1863 to 1864...............................Bradbury C. Hill.
1865 to 1866 ....Charles Moies.
1867 .....:..............................George C. Ballou.
1868 to 1869................................Lysander Flagg.
1870...Edward L. Freeman.

APPENDIX C.

LIST OF DEPUTIES AND REPRESENTATIVES IN THE GENERAL
ASSEMBLY FROM SMITHFIELD.

Deputies.

1731.

May Session,	Jonathan Sprague,	William Arnold.
October,	Capt. Silvanus Scott,	Daniel Jencks.

1732.

May,	Jonathan Sprague,	James Aldrich.
October,	James Aldrich,	Daniel Jencks.

1733.

May,	Daniel Jencks,	James Aldrich.
October,	same,	same.

1734.

May,	Daniel Jencks,	Capt. Joseph Mowry,
October,	Maj. William Smith,	·Daniel Jencks.

1735.

May,	Maj. William Smith,	James Aldrich.
October,	Maj. William Smith,	Daniel Jencks.

1736.

May,	Daniel Jencks,	Thomas Sayles.
October,	Maj. William Smith,	same.

1737.

May,	Thomas Sayles,	Daniel Jenckes.
October,	same,	same.

1738.

May,	Thomas Sayles,	William Arnold.
October,	Capt. Richard Sayles,	same.

1739.

May,	Resolved Waterman,	William Jenckes.
July,	same,	same.
October,	John Ballou,	Thomas Lapham.

1740.

| May, | Resolved Waterman, | Daniel Comstock. |
| October, | same, | same. |

1741.

| May, | Resolved Waterman, | John Sayles. |
| October, | same, | same. |

1742.

| May, | James Aldrich, | John Sayles. |
| October, | Daniel Jencks, | Thomas Steere. |

1743.

| May, | Thomas Steere, | David Comstock. |
| October, | Maj. William Smith, | Thomas Steere. |

1744.

| May, | Maj. William Smith, | Thomas Steere. |
| October, | David Comstock, | David Wilkinson. |

1745.

| May, | John Sayles, | Thomas Arnold. |
| October, | same, | same. |

1746.

| May, | Thomas Steere, | David Comstock. |
| October, | same, | same. |

1747.

| May, | Thomas Lapham, | Jonathan Arnold. |
| October, | same, | same. |

1748.

| May, | Jonathan Arnold, | Israel Wilkinson. |
| October, | same, | same. |

1749.

| May, | Thomas Lapham, | John Aldrich. |
| October, | Lieut. Thomas Arnold, | same. |

1750.

| May, | Thomas Lapham, | Lieut. Thomas Arnold. |
| October, | same, | John Aldrich. |

1751.

| May, | Thomas Arnold, | John Aldrich. |
| October. | Thoms Arnold, | same. |

1752.

| May, | Thomas Arnold, | John Aldrich. |
| October, | same, | Thomas Lapham. |

1753.

| May, | John Aldrich, | Thomas Owen. |
| October, | Thomas Arnold, | same. |

1754.

| May, | Thomas Arnold, | Jonathan Arnold. |
| October, | David Comstock, | John Aldrich. |

1755.

| May, | John Aldrich, | Jonathan Arnold. |
| October, | Jonathan Arnold, | Thomas Owen. |

1756.

| May, | Thomas Owen, | John Sayles, Jr. |
| October, | same. | same. |

1757.

| May, | Thomas Arnold, | Jeremiah Mowry. |
| October, | same. | same. |

1758.

| | Thomas Arnold, | Jeremiah Mowry. |

1759.

February,	Thomas Arnold,	Jeremiah Mowry.
May,	John Sayles, Jr.,	Joseph Mowry, Jr.
June,	Joseph Mowry, Jr.	
August,	John Sayles, Jr.,	Joseph Mowry, Jr.
October,	Thomas Arnold,	same.

1760.

February,	Thomas Arnold,	Joseph Mowry, Jr.
Day before general election—		
May,	Thomas Arnold,	same.
June,	same,	same.
August,	same,	same.
October,	Baulston Brayton,	Capt. Joseph Mowry.
December,	same,	same.

1761.

February,	Baulston Brayton,	Capt. Joseph Mowry.
March,	same,	same.
May,	same,	same.
June,	same,	same.
October,	same,	same.

1762.

February,	Thomas Arnold,	Baulston Brayton.
March special session, Thomas Arnold.		
May,	Thomas Arnold,	Jonathan Arnold.
June,	same,	same.
August,	same,	same.
September,	same,	same.
October,	same,	same.

1763.

February,	Thomas Arnold,	Jonathan Arnold.
May,	Caleb Aldrich,	Stephen Whipple.
June,	same,	same.
August,	Stephen Whipple.	
October,	Joseph Mowry,	Samuel Winsor.

1764.

January,	None.	
February,	Capt. Joseph Mowry,	Samuel Winsor.
May,	same,	same.
June,	Samuel Winsor.	
Special Session—		
July,	Capt. Joseph Mowry, Jr.,	Samuel Winsor.
September,	same,	same.
October,	David Comstock,	Samuel Winsor.
November,	same,	same.

1765.

May,	Thomas Steere,	Samuel Winsor.
June,	same,	same.
September,	same,	same.
October,	same,	Daniel Mowry, Jr.

1766.

February,	Thomas Steere,	Daniel Mowry, Jr.
May,	same,	same,
June,	same,	same,

September,	Thomas Steere,	Daniel Mowry, Jr.
October,	same,	same.
December,	same,	same.

1767.

May,	Samuel Winsor.	Stephen Whipple.
June, 2 Sessions,	same,	same.
August,	same,	same.

1768.

February,	Samuel Winsor,	John Farnum.
May,	Thomas Lapham,	Daniel Smith.
June,	same,	same.
September,	same,	same.

1769.

February,	Caleb Aldrich,	Daniel Mowry, Jr.
May,	same,	same.
June,	same,	same.
September,	same,	same.
October,	same,	Stephen Whipple.

1770.

May,	Caleb Aldrich,	Daniel Mowry, Jr.
June,	same,	same.
September,	same,	same.
October,	same,	same.

1771.

May,	Caleb Aldrich,	Daniel Mowry, Jr.
June,	same,	same.
August,	same,	same.
October,	Daniel Mowry, Jr.,	Welcome Arnold.

1772.

May,	Welcome Arnold.	
August,	Samuel Winsor,	Welcome Arnold.
October,	same,	Daniel Mowry, Jr.
December,	same,	same.

1773.

January,	Samuel Winsor,	Daniel Mowry, Jr.
May,	Daniel Mowry, Jr.,	Capt. Jonathan Arnold.
August,	same,	same.
October,	Israel Wilkinson,	William Winsor.

22

1774.

May,	Israel Wilkinson,	William Winsor.
June,	same,	same,
August,	same,	same.
October,	same,	same.
December, Special,	same,	same.

1775.

April, Special,	Israel Wilkinson.	
May,	Daniel Mowry, Jr.,	Stephen Whipple.
June,	same,	same.
August,	same,	same.
October,	Arnold Paine,	same.

1776.

January,	Arnold Paine,	Stephen Whipple.
February,	same,	same.
March,	same,	same.
May,	Daniel Mowry, Jr.,	Capt. Andrew Waterman.
June,	same,	same.
July,	same,	same.
August,	same,	same.
September,	same,	same.
October,	Daniel Mowry, Jr.	
Special—		
November,	Daniel Mowry, Jr.,	Capt. Andrew Waterman,
December,	same.	

1777.

February,	Daniel Mowry, Jr.,	Capt. Andrew Waterman.
March,	same,	same.
April,	same,	same.
May,	Samuel Winsor,	
2d Session—		
May,	Samuel Winsor,	Ezekiel Angell.
June,	same,	same.
July, Special,	same,	same.
August,	same,	same.
September,	same,	
October,	Caleb Aldrich,	Peleg Arnold.
December,	same,	same.
Special Session—		
December,	same,	same.

1778.

February,	Peleg Arnold.	
March,	Caleb Aldrich,	Peleg Arnold.
May,	same,	same.
May, Special,	same,	same.
June,	same,	same.
September,	Caleb Aldrich,	
October,	Daniel Mowry,	Caleb Aldrich.
December,	same,	same.

1779.

Special—		
January,	Daniel Mowry,	Caleb Aldrich.
February,	same,	same.
May,	Andrew Waterman,	Jonathan Comstock.
June,	Andrew Waterman.	
August,	same,	same.
September,	same,	same.
October,	Sylvanus Sayles,	same.
December,	same,	same.

1780.

| February, | Sylvanus Sayles. | |
| March Special, | same, | Jonathan Comstock. |

1781.

January,	Elisha Mowry,	Edward Thompson.
February,	same,	same.
March,	same,	same.
2d Session—		
May,	Andrew Waterman,	Henry Jenckes.
Special Session—		
July,	same,	same.
August,	same,	same.
October,	Stephen Arnold.	
December,	same.	

1782.

January,	Luke Arnold,	Stephen Arnold.
Special Session—		
February,	same,	same.
May,	William Waterman,	Peleg Arnold.
June,	same,	same.
August,	same,	same.

| October, | Elisha Mowry, | Peleg Arnold. |
| November, | same, | same. |

1783.

February,	Elisha Mowry,	Peleg Arnold.
May,	same,	Stephen Arnold, Jr.
June,	same,	same.
October,	Stephen Arnold,	William Waterman.
December,	Stephen Arnold, Jr.	

1784.

February,	Stephen Arnold, Jr.,	William Waterman.
May,	Stephen Arnold,	Elisha Mowry.
June,	same,	same.
August,	same.	
October,	Stephen Arnold, Jr.,	William Aldrich.

1785.

February,	Stephen Arnold, Jr.,	William Aldrich.
May,	same,	same.
June,	same,	same.
August,	Stephen Arnold.	
October,	Stephen Arnold, Jr.,	Daniel Mowry, Jr.

1786.

February,	Stephen Arnold, Jr.,	Daniel Mowry.
March,	Stephen Arnold,	same.
May,		
June,	John Sayles,	Andrew Waterman.
August,	same,	same.
October,	same,	same.
December,	same,	same.

1787.

March,	John Sayles,	Andrew Waterman.
May,	same,	same.
June,	same,	same,
Special Session—		
September,	same,	same.
October,	same,	same.

1788.

February,	John Sayles,	Andrew Waterman,
March,	same,	same,
May,	same,	same.

June,	Andrew Waterman,	
October,	John Sayles,	Andrew Waterman,
December,	same,	same.

1789.

March,	John Sayles,	Andrew Waterman.
May,	same,	same.
June,	same,	same.
September,	same,	same.
October,	same,	same.
Oct. 2d session,	same,	Stephen Whipple.

1790.

January,	John Sayles,	Stephen Whipple.
May,	same,	Mr. Job Aldrich.
June,	same,	same.
September,	same,	same.
October,	same,	same.

1791.

February,	John Sayles,	Job Aldrich.
May,	same,	same,
June,	same,	same,
October,	Daniel Mowry,	same.

1792.

February,	Daniel Mowry,	Job Aldrich.
May,	John Smith,	Arnold Paine.
June,	same,	same.
August,	same,	same.
October,	same.	same.

1793.

February,	John Smith,	Arnold Paine.
May,	John Smith, Jr.,	same.
June,	same,	same.
October,	Arnold Paine,	Henry Jenckes.

1794.

February,	Arnold Paine,	Henry Jenckes.
March,	same,	same.
May,	same,	same.
June,	John Paine,	same.
October,	same,	same.

1795.

January,	John Paine.	
May,	same,	Henry Jenckes.
June,	same,	same.
October,	Job Aldrich,	Joshua Jenckes.

1796.

February,	Job Aldrich,	Joshua Jenckes.
May,	same,	same.
June,	same,	same.
October,	same.	same.

Representatives.

1797.

February,	Job Aldrich,	Joshua Jenckes.
May,	same,	same.
June,	same,	same.
October,	same,	same.
December,	same,	same.

1798.

January,	Job Aldrich,	Joshua Jenckes.
May,	same.	William Mowry.
June,	same,	same.
October,	same,	same.

1799.

February,	Job Aldrich,	William Mowry.
May,	William Mowry,	Ezekiel Comstock,
June,	same,	same.
October,	same,	same.

1800.

February,	William Mowry,	Ezekiel Comstock,
May,	same,	same.
June,	same,	same.
October,	same,	Thomas Mann,

1801.

February,	William Mowry,	Thomas Mann.
May,	same,	same.
June,	same,	same.
October,	same,	same.

1802.

February,	William Mowry,	Thomas Mann,
May,	Robert Harris,	same.
June,	same,	same.
October,	same,	same.

1803.

February,	Robert Harris,	Thomas Mann.
May, 2 sessions,	same,	same.
October,	same,	same.

1804.

February,	Robert Harris,	Thomas Mann.
May,	same,	same.
June,	same,	same.
October,	same,	same.

1805.

February,	Robert Harris,	Thomas Mann.
May,	same,	same.
June,	same,	same.
October,	same,	same.

1806.

February,	Robert Harris,	Thomas Mann,
May,	same,	same.
June,	same,	Enos Mowry.
October,	same,	same.

1807.

February,	Robert Harris,	Enos Mowry.
May,	same,	Daniel Angell.
June,	same,	same.
October,	same,	same.

1808.

February,	Robert Harris,	Enos Mowry.
May,	same,	same.
June,	same,	same.
October.	same,	same.

1809.

February,	Robert Harris,	Enos Mowry.
March,	same,	same.
May,	same,	John Angell, Jr.,
June,	same,	same.
October,	Daniel Mowry, Jr.,	Isaac Wilkinson.

1810.

February,	Daniel Mowry, Jr.,	Isaac Wilkinson,
May,	Isaac Wilkinson,	Daniel Angell.
June,	Daniel Angell.	
October,	Isaac Wilkinson.	Daniel Angell.

1811.

February,	Isaac Wilkinson,	Daniel Angell.
May,	same,	same.
June,	same,	same.
October,	Thomas Mann,	same.

1812.

February,	Thomas Mann,	Daniel Angell.
May,	same,	same.
June,	same,	same.
July, special session,	same,	same.
October,	same,	Benjamin Hall,

1813.

February,	Thomas Mann,	Benjamin Hall,
May,	same,	same.
June,	same,	same.
October,	same,	same.

1814.

February,	Thomas Mann,	Benjamin Hall,
May,	same,	same.
June,	same,	same.
Sept., special,	same.	
October,	same,	Elisha Steere.

1815.

February,	Thomas Mann,	Elisha Steere.
May,	Elisha Steere.	
June,	same.	
October,	same,	Marcus Arnold.

1816.

February,	Elisha Steere,	Marcus Arnold.
May,	same.	
June,	same.	
October,	same,	Isaac Wilkinson.

1817.

February,	Elisha Steere.	
May,	Isaac Wilkinson,	Nathan B. Sprague.
June,	same,	same.
October,	Peleg Arnold,	same.

1818.

February,	Nathan B. Sprague.	
May,	Peleg Arnold,	Nathan B. Sprague.
June,	same,	same.
October,	same,	same.

1819.

February,	Nathan B. Sprague,	
May,	same,	Nathan Aldrich.
June,	same,	same.
October,	same,	same.

1820.

February,	Nathan B. Sprague,	Nathan Aldrich.
May,	same,	same.
June,	same,	same.
October,	same,	Daniel Angell.

1821. Special session.

January,	Nathan B. Sprague,	Daniel Angell.
February,	same,	same.
May,	Daniel Winsor,	Daniel Angell.
June.	same,	same.
October,	same,	same.

1822.

January,	Daniel Winsor,	Daniel Angell.
May,	Daniel Angell.	Nathan B. Sprague,
June,	same,	same.
October,	Nathan B. Sprague,	Nathan Aldrich.

1823.

January,	Nathan B. Sprague.	Nathan Aldrich.
May,	same,	same.
June,	same,	same.
October,	same,	same.

23

1824.

January,	Nathan B. Sprague,	Nathan Aldrich.
May,	same,	same.
May, 2d session,	same,	
October,	same,	Nathan Aldrich.

1825.

January,	Nathan B. Sprague.	
May,	same,	Arnold Spear.
June,	same,	same.
October,	same.	same.

1826.

January,	Nathan B. Sprague,	Arnold Spear.
May,	same,	same.
June,	same,	same.
October,	same.	same.

Representatives.

1824.

Nathan B. Sprague.

1825.

| Nathan B. Sprague, | Arnold Spear. |

1826.

| Nathan B. Sprague, | Arnold Spear. |

1827.

| Nathan B. Sprague, | Arnold Spear. |

1828.

| Arnold Spear. | Stephen Steere. |

1829.

| Stephen Steere, | Morton Mowry. |

1830.

| Stephen Steere, | Morton Mowry. |

1831.

| Elisha Smith, | Ezekiel Fowler. |

1832.

| Elisha Smith, | Ezekiel Fowler. |

1833.

Ezekiel Fowler,   Daniel Wilkinson.

1834.

Arnold Spear,   Daniel G. Harris.

1835.

Ezekiel Fowler,   Sessions Mowry.

1836.

May,	Sessions Mowry,	John Paine.
June,	Isaac Wilkinson.	Asa Winsor.
October.	same,	same.

1837.

January,	Isaac Wilkinson,	Asa Winsor.
May,	same,	same.
June,	same,	same.
October,	Sessions Mowry,	Nathan Andrews.

1838.

January.		
May,	Sessions Mowry,	Samuel Clarke.
June,	same,	same.
October,	same,	same.

1839.

January,	Sessions Mowry,	Samuel Clarke.
May,	same,	same.
June,	same,	same.
October,	same,	same.

1840.

Sessions Mowry,   Samuel Clarke.

1841.

Sessions Mowry,   Samuel Clarke.

1842.

Sessions Mowry,   Samuel Clarke.

1843.

Thomas Buffum,	Richard Mowry,	Jonathan Cole,
David Wilbur,	James Harkness,	Pardon Angell.

1844.

George C. Ballou,	Elisha Steere,	George Aldrich,
Bradbury C. Hill,	Charles Moies,	Nathan Spalding.

1845.

Thomas Buffum,   Elisha Smith,   Gideon Bradford,
Robert Harris,   James Harkness,   Nelson B. Jencks.

1846.

Thomas Buffum,   Emor H. Smith,   Gideon Bradford,
James Harkness,   Robert Harris,   Nelson B. Jencks.

1847.

Thomas Buffum,   Emor H. Smith,
Gideon Bradford,   James Harkness.

1848.

Daniel Pearce,   John Fenner,   Amasa Smith,
Israel Sayles,   Alden Coe,   Edwin W. Mowry.

1849.

Thomas Buffum,   Robert Harris,   John Fenner,
Israel Sayles,   Henry Gooding,   George B. Aldrich.

1850.

Robert Harris,   Israel Sayles,   Samuel S. Mallory,
Emor H. Smith,   Earl A. Wright,   Emor Coe.

1851.

Thomas Buffum,   Daniel Pearce,   John Fenner,
Earl A. Wright,   James Phetteplace,   Israel B. Purinton.

1852.

Robert Harris,   Daniel Pearce,   John Fenner,
Thomas Steere,   Elisha Mowry, 2d,   Israel B. Purinton.

1853.

Israel Sayles,   John Fenner,   Emor Coe,
Thomas Steere,   Elisha Mowry, 2d,   Samuel D. Slocum.

1854.

Edwin Harris,   Henry Gooding,   Smith R. Mowry,
Edwin W. Mowry,   Elisha Mowry, 2d,   Henry S. Pearce.

1855.

Nathaniel Spaulding,   Charles Moies,   Jeremiah J. Young,
Ansel Holman,   Daniel T. Eddy,   Henry G. Pearce.

1856.

Lysander Flagg,	Ansel Holman,	Henry G. Pearce,
Nathaniel Spaulding,	William P. Steere,	Jeremiah J. Young.

1857.

Lysander Flagg,	Jonathan Barnes,	James H. Chace,
Nathaniel Spaulding,	William P. Steere,	Sullivan Ballou.

1858.

Lysander Flagg,	Jonathan Barnes,	William Newell,
Nathaniel Spaulding,	William P. Steere,	Sullivan Ballou.

1859.

James A. Barnes,	Harris M. Irons,	Daniel Mowry,
Jabez W. Mowry,	William Newell,	Albert C. Vose.

1860.

James A. Barnes,	Bradbury C. Hill,	Simon S. Steere,
Jabez W. Mowry,	William Newell,	Albert C. Vose.

1861.

Bailies Bourne,	Bradbury C. Hill,	Harris M. Irons,
Jabez W. Mowry,	William Newell,	Carlisle Vose,

1862.

Bradbury C. Hill,	Carlisle Vose,	William Newell,
Jabez W. Mowry,	Joseph Olney,	Simon S. Steere.

1863.

David Ballou,	Carlisle Vose,	Stafford W. Razee,
Jabez W. Mowry,	Joseph Olney,	Harris M. Irons.

1864.

Joseph Olney,	Stafford W. Razee,	George W. Holt,
Anthony Steere,	Lyman A. Taft,	Daniel Sayles,

1865.

Daniel R. Ballou,	Horace Daniels,	George W. Holt,
Simon B. Mowry,	Spencer Mowry,	William T. Smith.

1866.

Daniel R. Ballou,	Elisha W. Brown,	Benjamin Comstock,
Benjamin F. Greene,	Elmer N. Maynard,	Spencer Mowry.

1867.

| Daniel R. Ballou, | Lysander Flagg, | Benjamin Comstock, |
| Jabez W. Mowry, | Spencer Mowry, | Obed Paine. |

1868.

| Elmer N. Maynard, | Arlon Mowry, | Obed Paine, |
| Benjamin Comstock, | Edward L. Freeman, | Jabez W. Mowry. |

1869.

| Jabez W. Mowry, | Arlon Mowry, | Baylies Bourne, |
| Edward L. Freeman, | William H. Seagraves, | William D. Aldrich. |

1870.

| Jabez W. Mowry, | Arlon Mowry, | William H. Seagraves. |
| William D. Aldrich, | Edward A. Brown, | Cyrus Arnold. |

APPENDIX D

TOWN COUNCIL.

1731.

President: John Arnold.

Joseph Mowry, Thomas Steere, Samuel Aldrich,
John Mowry, Benjamin Smith.

1732.

President: John Arnold.

Joseph Mowry, John Mowry, Elisha Smith,
Thomas Shippy, Thomas Sayles.

1733.

President: Major William Smith.

Joseph Mowry, Joseph Arnold, Thomas Shippy,
James Aldrich, John Dexter.

1734.

President: Thomas Steere.

Joseph Mowry, Joseph Arnold, Thomas Shippy,
Thomas Smith, Jr., John Dexter.

1735.

President: Major William Smith.

Joseph Arnold, James Aldrich, Job Whipple,
David Comstock, John Brown.

1736.

President: Major William Smith.

John Whipple, David Comstock, John Brown,
Lieut. Joseph Smith, Benjamin Pain.

1737.

President: Thomas Sayles.

William Arnold,   John Brown,   Thomas Steere,
     Benjamin Pain,   John Dexter.

1738.

President: Thomas Sayles.

William Arnold,   John Brown,   Thomas Steere,
     Benjamin Pain,   John Dexter.

1739.

President: Thomas Steere.

Thomas Shippy,   John Brown,   John Dexter,
     Jonathan Arnold,   William Jenckes.

1740.

President: Thomas Steere.

Thomas Shippy,   John Brown,   John Dexter,
     Jonathan Arnold,   William Jenckes.

1741.

President: Thomas Steere.

Thomas Shippy,   John Brown,   John Dexter,
     Jonathan Arnold,   William Jenckes.

1742.

President: Thomas Steere.

Thomas Shippy,   John Brown,   John Dexter,
     Jonathan Arnold,   William Jenckes.

1743.

President: Thomas Steere.

Thomas Shippy,   John Brown,   John Dexter,
     Jonathan Arnold,   William Jenckes.

1744.

President: Thomas Steere.

Thomas Shippy,   John Brown,   John Dexter,
     Jonathan Arnold, Jr.,   William Jenckes.

1745.

President: Thomas Steere.

Thomas Shippy,   David Comstock,   Israel Wilkinson,
     Jonathan Arnold,   William Jenckes.

1746.

President: Thomas Steere.

Thomas Shippy,   David Comstock,   Israel Wilkinson,
   Jonathan Arnold,   William Jenckes.

1747.

President: Joseph Smith.

Jeremiah Mowry,   Robert Staples,   Thomas Owen,
   Capt. Daniel Mowry,   John Aldrich.

1748.

President: Lieut. Thomas Arnold.

Thomas Owen,   John Aldrich,   John Jenckes,
   Capt. Daniel Mowry,   Benjamin Arnold.

1749.

President: Thomas Steere.

Thomas Owen,   John Aldrich,   John Jenckes,
   Capt. Daniel Mowry,   Benjamin Arnold.

1750.

President: Thomas Steere.

John Aldrich,   Dr. John Jenckes,   Capt. Daniel Mowry,
   Baulston Brayton,   Preserved Harris.

1751.

President: Thomas Steere.

John Aldrich,   Dr. John Jenckes.   Capt. Daniel Mowry,
   Baulston Brayton,   Preserved Harris.

1752.

President: Thomas Steere.

John Aldrich,   Dr. John Jenckes,   Capt. Daniel Mowry,
   Baulston Brayton,   Preserved Harris.

1753.

President: Thomas Steere.

John Aldrich,   Dr. John Jenckes,   Capt. Daniel Mowry,
   Baulston Brayton,   Preserved Harris.

1754.

President: Thomas Steere.

John Aldrich,   Dr. John Jenckes,   Capt. Daniel Mowry,
   David Comstock,   Preserved Harris.
24

1755.

President: Thomas Steere.

John Aldrich,   Dr. John Jenckes,   John Sayles,
     David Comstock,   Preserved Harris.

1756.

President: Thomas Steere.

John Aldrich,   Dr. John Jenckes,   Capt. Daniel Mowry,
     David Comstock,   Preserved Harris.

1757.

President: Thomas Steere.

John Aldrich,   Dr. John Jenckes,   Capt. Daniel Mowry,
     David Comstock,   Preserved Harris.

1758.

President: Thomas Steere.

John Aldrich,   Dr. John Jenckes,   Capt. Daniel Mowry,
     David Comstock,   Preserved Harris.

1759.

President: Thomas Steere.

John Aldrich,   Dr. John Jenckes,   Capt. Daniel Mowry,
     David Comstock,   Preserved Harris.

1760.

President: Thomas Steere.

John Aldrich,   Dr. John Jenckes,   Capt. Daniel Mowry,
     David Comstock,   Preserved Harris.

1761.

President: Thomas Steere.

Ezekiel Angell,   William Jenckes,   Capt. Daniel Mowry,
     David Comstock,   Preserved Harris.

1762.

President: Thomas Steere.

Ezekiel Angell,   William Jenckes,   Capt. Daniel Mowry,
     David Comstock,   Preserved Harris.

1763.

President: Thomas Steere.

Ezekiel Angell,   William Jenckes,   Capt. Daniel Mowry,
     David Comstock,   Preserved Harris.

1764.

President: Thomas Steere.

Ezekiel Angell,   William Jenckes,   Capt. Daniel Mowry,
David Comstock,   Preserved Harris.

1765.

President: Thomas Steere.

Ezekiel Angell,   William Jenckes,   Capt. Daniel Mowry,
David Comstock,   Preserved Harris.

1766.

President: Thomas Steere.

Ezekiel Angell,   Thomas Lapham,   Capt. Daniel Mowry,
David Comstock,   Preserved Harris.

1767.

President: Thomas Steere.

Ezekiel Angell,   ·   Thomas Lapham,   Capt. Daniel Mowry,
Stephen Arnold,   Preserved Harris.

1768.

President: Thomas Steere.

John Sayles,   Thomas Lapham,   Caleb Aldrich,
Stephen˜Arnold,   Preserved Harris.

1769.

President: Thomas Steere.

John Sayles,   Thomas Lapham,   Caleb Aldrich,
Stephen Arnold,   Preserved Harris.

1770.

President: Thomas Steere.

John Sayles,   Thomas Lapham,   Caleb Aldrich,
Stephen Arnold,   Preserved Harris.

1771.

President: Thomas Steere.

John Sayles,   Thomas Lapham,   Caleb Aldrich,
Stephen Arnold,   Preserved Harris.

1772.

President: Thomas Steere.

John Sayles,   Caleb Aldrich,   Stephen Arnold,
Preserved Harris,   Stephen Whipple.

1773.

President: John Sayles.

Caleb Aldrich,   Preserved Harris,   Job Aldrich.

1774.

President: Ezekiel Comstock.

Caleb Aldrich,   Job Aldrich,   Abraham Mathewson,
Henry Jenckes,   Jonathan Gulley.

1775.

President: Ezekiel Comstock.

Job Aldrich,   Abraham Mathewson, Henry Jenckes,
Jonathan Gulley,   Jeremiah Harris.

1776.

President: Ezekiel Comstock.

Job Aldrich,   Abraham Mathewson, Henry Jenckes,
Jonathan Gulley.   John Man.

1777.

President: Henry Jenckes.

Daniel Smith,   John Man,   Stephen Brayton,
Jonathan Comstock,   Stephen Arnold.

1778.

President: Henry Jenckes.

Daniel Smith,   John Man,   Stephen Brayton,
Sylvanus Sayles,   Stephen Arnold.

1779.

President: Capt. Sylvanus Sayles.

John Man,   Stephen Arnold,   Edward Thompson,
William Waterman,   Arnold Pain.

1780.

President: Caleb Aldrich.

John Man,   Stephen Whipple,   Edward Thompson,
Arnold Pain,   Job Aldrich.

1781.

President: Caleb Aldrich.

John Man,   Stephen Whipple,   Edward Thompson,
Arnold Pain,   Abraham Mathewson.

1782.

President: Caleb Aldrich.

Stephen Whipple, Edward Thompson, Arnold Pain,
Abraham Mathewson, John Angell.

1783.

President: Caleb Aldrich.

Jesse Jenckes, Edward Thompson, Arnold Pain,
John Angell, James Smith.

1784.

President: Caleb Aldrich.

Jesse Jenckes, Edward Thompson, Arnold Pain,
John Angell, James Smith.

1785.

President: Daniel Mowry, Jr.

Jesse Jenckes, Stephen Whipple, John Angell,
James Smith, Philip Mowry.

1786.

President: Daniel Mowry, Jr.

Jesse Jenckes, James Smith, Philip Mowry, Jr.,
John Man, Jr., Robert Latham.

1787.

President: Daniel Mowry, Jr.

Jesse Jenckes, James Smith, Philip Mowry, Jr.,
John Man, Jr., Robert Latham.

1788.

President: Daniel Mowry, Jr.

Jesse Jenckes, James Smith, Philip Mowry, Jr.,
John Man, Jr., Robert Latham.

1789.

President: William Waterman.

Jesse Jenckes, James Appleby, Arnold Pain,
John Man, Jr., Robert Lathan.

1790.

President: Joseph Farnum.

Jesse Jenckes, James Appleby, Arnold Pain,
John Man, Jr., Emor Smith.

1791.

President: Joseph Farnum.

Jesse Jenckes,   James Appleby,   Arnold Pain,
    John Man, Jr.,   Emor Smith.

1792.

President: George Comstock.

Jesse Jenckes,   James Appleby,   Arnold Pain,
    John Man, Jr.,   Joseph Mowry.

1793.

President: George Comstock.

Jesse Jenckes,   James Appleby,   Arnold Pain,
    John Man, Jr.,   Joseph Mowry,

1794.

President: Capt. Sylvanus Sayles.

Samuel Clark,   Job Aldrich,   Thomas Aldrich,
    Elisha Olney,   Philip Mowry.

1795.

President: Capt. Sylvanus Sayles.

Samuel Clark,   Job Aldrich,   Thomas Aldrich,
    Elisha Olney,   Philip Mowry.

1796.

President: Capt. Sylvanus Sayles.

Samuel Clark,   Duty Winsor,   Daniel Smith, Jr.,
    John Man, Jr.,   Ezekiel Comstock.

1797.

President: Samuel Clark.

Duty Winsor,   John Man,   Ezekiel Comstock,
    Israel Taft,   Seth Mowry.

1798.

President: Samuel Clark.

Duty Winsor,   John Man,   Ezekiel Comstock,
    Israel Taft,   Seth Mowry.

1799.

President: Samuel Clark.

Edward Medbury,   John Man,   John Jenckes,
John Pain,   Seth Mowry,   Elisha Olney.

1800.

President: Duty Winsor.

| Edward Medbury, | John Man, | John Jenckes, |
| John Pain, | Seth Mowry, | Ahab Mowry. |

1801.

President: John Jenckes.

| John Man, | Seth Mowry, | Ahab Mowry, |
| Richard Buffum, | Daniel Winsor, | Elijah Arnold. |

1802.

President: Thomas Mann.

| Seth Mowry, | Ahab Mowry, | Richard Buffum, |
| Daniel Winsor, | None, | No sixth councilman. |

1803.

President: Thomas Mann.

| Seth Mowry, | Richard Buffum, | Samuel Hill, Jr., |
| Enos Mowry, | Elijah Derry, | Job Arnold. |

1804.

President: Thomas Mann.

| Seth Mowry, | Stephen Buffum, | Samuel Hill, Jr., |
| Enos Mowry, | Thomas Appleby, | William Aldrich. |

1805.

President: Thomas Mann.

| Seth Mowry, | Samuel Hill, Jr., | Enos Mowry, |
| Job Arnold, | Thomas Buffum, | Benjamin Hall. |

1806.

President: Samuel Hill.

| Seth Mowry, | Enos Mowry, | Job Arnold, |
| Thomas Buffum, | Benjamin Hall, | David Harris. |

1807.

President: Samuel Hill.

| Elisha Steere, | Enos Mowry, | Job Arnold, |
| Nathan Aldrich, | Benjamin Hall, | David Harris. |

1808.

President: Samuel Hill.

| Elisha Steere, | Enos Mowry, | Job Arnold, |
| Nathan Aldrich, | Benjamin Hall, | David Harris. |

1809.

President: Thomas Mann.

Elisha Steere,	Nathan Aldrich,	Benjamin Hall,
David Harris,	Thomas Appleby,	Daniel Angell.

1810.

President: Thomas Mann.

Elisha Steere,	Nathan Aldrich,	Benjamin Hall,
Daniel Harris,	Thomas Appleby,	Daniel Angell.

1811.

President: Thomas Mann.

Elisha Steere,	Benjamin Hall,	David Harris,
James Appleby,	Daniel Angell,	Stephen Buffum.

1812.

President: Thomas Mann.

Elisha Steere,	Benjamin Hall,	David Harris,
James Appleby,	Daniel Angell,	Stephen Buffum.

1813.

President: Thomas Mann.

Elisha Steere,	Benjamin Hall,	David Harris,
James Appleby,	Daniel Angell,	Stephen Buffum.

1814.

President: Benjamin Hall.

Elisha Steere,	James Appleby,	Daniel Angell,
Stephen Buffum,	None,	None.

1815.

President: Thomas Buffum.

Daniel Angell,	David Tucker,	Marcus Arnold,
Thomas Angell,	Arnold Jenckes,	Jeremiah Smith.

1816.

President: Daniel Angell.

Thomas Angell,	Arnold Jenckes,	Jeremiah Smith, Jr.,
Reuben Mowry,	David Wilkinson,	Stephen Steere.

1817.

President: Daniel Angell.

Thomas Angell,	Jeremiah Smith, Jr.,	Reuben Mowry,
David Wilkinson,	Stephen Steere,	William Aldrich.

1818.

President: Reuben Mowry.

David Wilkinson,	Stephen Steere,	William Aldrich,
Winsor Aldrich,		

1819.

President: Reuben Mowry.

David Wilkinson,	Stephen Steere,	William Aldrich,
Winsor Aldrich,	Morton Mowry,	Daniel Winsor.

1820.

President: Reuben Mowry.

David Wilkinson,	Stephen Steere,	William Aldrich,
Winsor Aldrich,	Morton Mowry,	Arnold Spear.

1821.

President: Reuben Mowry.

David Wilkinson,	Stephen Steere,	George Chace,
Winsor Aldrich,	Morton Mowry,	Arnold Spear.

1822.

President: Daniel Angell.

David Wilkinson,	Morton Mowry,	Arnold Spear,
George Chace,	Jeremiah Whipple,	Abraham Winsor.

1823.

President: Thomas Buffum.

David Wilkinson,	Morton Mowry,	Arnold Spear,
Cyrus Arnold,	Jeremiah Whipple,	Abraham Winsor.

1824.

President: David Wilkinson.

Morton Mowry,	Charles Appleby,	Jeremiah Whipple,
Abraham Winsor,	Barney Dodge,	Samuel B. Harris.

1825.

President: Samuel B. Harris.

Morton Mowry,	Charles Appleby,	Jeremiah Whipple,
Abraham Winsor,	Barney Dodge,	Lewis Dexter.

1826.

President: Samuel B. Harris.

Morton Mowry,	Nathaniel Mowry,	Jeremiah Whipple,
Barney Dodge,	Lewis Dexter,	Sessions Mowry.

25

1827.

President: Morton Mowry.

Nathaniel Mowry,	Jeremiah Whipple,	Barney Dodge,
Lewis Dexter,	Sessions Mowry,	David Lapham.

1828.

President: Morton Mowry.

Nathaniel Mowry,	Jeremiah Whipple,	Barney Dodge,
Lewis Dexter,	Sessions Mowry,	David Lapham.

1829.

President: Morton Mowry.

Nathaniel Mowry,	Jeremiah Whipple,	Barney Dodge,
Lewis Dexter,	Sessions Mowry,	David Lapham.

1830.

President: Lewis Dexter.

Sessions Mowry,	David Lapham,	Elisha Smith,
Richard S. Scott,	Wilder Holbrook,	Elisha Olney, Jr.

1831.

President: Lewis Dexter.

Elisha Smith,	Richard S. Scott,	Wilder Holbrook,
Elisha Olney, Jr.,	Daniel G. Harris,	George Chace.

1832.

President: Lewis Dexter.

Elisha Smith,	Richard S. Scott,	Wilder Holbrook.
Elisha Olney, Jr.,	None,	None.

1833.

President: Lewis Dexter.

Simon Aldrich,	Richard S. Scott,	Stephen Sheldon,
Asa W. Ballou,	Job S. Man,	Andrew Waterman.

1834.

President:

Stephen Sheldon,	Job S. Man,	Andrew Weatherhead,
Waterman F. Brown,	John Jenckes,	Edwin Harris.

1835.

President: Morton Mowry.

Stephen Sheldon,	Job S. Man,	Dexter Aldrich,
Asahel Phetteplace,	Samuel Clark,	Asahel Angell.

1836.

President: Morton Mowry.

Stephen Sheldon,	Cyrus Arnold,	Tyler Mowry,
Asahel Phetteplace,	Smith B. Mowry,	Asahel Angell.

1837.

President: Morton Mowry.

Stephen Sheldon,	Cyrus Arnold,	Samuel Clark,
Asahel Phetteplace,	Smith B. Mowry,	Asahel Angell.

1838.

President: Morton Mowry.

Samuel Clark,	Asahel Angell	Stephen Steere,
Dexter Aldrich,	Barney Dodge,	Uriah Benedict.

1839.

President: Morton Mowry.

Samuel Clark,	Asahel Angell,	Stephen Sheldon,
Dexter Aldrich,	Barney Dodge,	Burrill Aldrich.

1840.

President: Morton Mowry.

Samuel Clark,	Asahel Angell,	Barney Dodge,
Alvin Jenks,	Stephen Smith, 2d,	Pelatiah Metcalf.

1841.

President: Samuel Clark.

Dexter Aldrich,	Barney Dodge,	Alvin Jenks,
Stephen Smith, 2d,	Pelatiah Metcalf,	John Foster.

1842.

President: Arnold Spear.

Dexter Aldrich,	Alvin Jenks,	John Foster,
James T. Harkness,	Gideon Mowry,	Lyman Cook.

1843.

President: Arnold Spear.

Ahaz Mowry, Jr.,	Elisha Smith,	Daniel Sayles, Jr.,
Edward Evans,	Avery Gilman,	Benjamin Harris,
William M. Farnum,	Robert Harris,	Bradford Bullock.

1844.

President: Lewis Dexter.

John Foster,	Gideon Mowry,	Lyman Cook,
Christopher W. Kelly,	Lyman Wilmarth,	Ansel Holman.

1845.

President: Thomas Buffum.

Daniel Sayles,   Daniel Wilbur,   James Phetteplace,
Bradford Bullock,   Johnson G. Horton,   William M. Farnum.

1846.

President: Thomas Buffum.

Bradford Bullock,   David Wilbur,   James Phetteplace,
Albert Cook,   Horace Trowbridge,   William M. Farnum.

1847.

President: Thomas Buffum.

Daniel Pierce,   Benjamin Harris,   John Fenner,
Israel Wilkinson,   Israel Sayles,   Albert Cook.

1848.

President: Thomas Buffum.

Daniel Pierce,   Robert Harris,   Richard Mowry,
Israel Sayles,   John Knight,   Asa Winsor.

1849.

President: Thomas Buffum.

Robert Harris,   Richard Mowry,   Israel Sayles,
John Knight,   Thomas Latham,   Israel B. Purinton.

1850.

President: Thomas Buffum.

Robert Harris,   Israel Sayles,   John Knight,
Thomas Latham,   Alfred Allen,   William Smith.

1851.

President: Robert Harris.

Israel Sayles,   John Knight,   Thomas Lapham,
Samuel S. Mallory,   Alden Coe,   George B. Aldrich.

1852.

President: Robert Harris.

Thomas Latham,   Richard Smith,   Albert Cook,
John J. Carpenter,   John Knight.   ?

1853.

President: Robert Harris.

Thomas Latham,   Richard Smith,   Albert Cook,
John J. Carpenter,   John Knight.   ?

1854.

President: Richard Mowry.

Henry Stone,	James Phetteplace,	John B. Tallman,
Daniel Mowry,	Louis Aldrich,	Henry Gooding.

1855.

President: Daniel N. Paine.

John J. Carpenter,	James Phetteplace,	Harris M. Irons,
Daniel Mowry,	William Patt,	James H. Chace,

1856.

President: Lewis Dexter.

John J. Carpenter,	Harris M. Irons,	Daniel Mowry,
William Patt,	Charles Moies,	Harden Knight.

1857.

President: Lewis Dexter.

John J. Carpenter,	Harris M. Irons,	George Johnson,
William Patt,	Charles Moies,	Harden Knight.

1858.

President: Lewis Dexter.

John J. Carpenter,	Harris M. Irons,	George Johnson,
William Patt,	Charles Moies,	Daniel Mowry.

1859.

President: Lewis Dexter.

Charles Moies,	John J. Carpenter,	George Johnson,
Arlon Mowry,	William P. Steere, .	William Mowry.

1860.

President: Lewis Dexter.

Charles Moies,	John J. Carpenter,	George Johnson,
Arlon Mowry,	William P. Steere,	William Mowry.

1861.

President: Charles Moies.

Arlon Mowry,	William Mowry,	George M. Appleby,
George Johnson,	Harvey S. Bartlett,	John N. Spaulding.

1862.

President: Charles Moies.

Arlon Mowry,	William Mowry,	Wm. Duane Aldrich,
George Johnson,	Harvey S. Bartlett,	John N. Spaulding.

1863.

President: Charles Moies.

| Arlon Mowry, | William Mowry, | Wm. Duane Aldrich, |
| George Johnson, | William P. Steere, | John J. Carpenter. |

1864.

President: Charles Moies.

| Arlon Mowry, | William Mowry, | Wm. Duane Aldrich, |
| George Johnson, | William P. Steere, | Benjamin Comstock. |

1865.

President: Charles Moies.

| Arlon Mowry, | William Mowry, | Wm. Duane Aldrich, |
| George Johnson, | William P. Steere, | Benjamin Comstock. |

1866.

President: Charles Moies.

| Arlon Mowry, | William Mowry, | Wm. Duane Aldrich, |
| George Johnson, | William P. Steere, | Baylies Bourne. |

1867.

President: Charles Moies.

| Arlon Mowry, | William Mowry, | Wm. Duane Aldrich, |
| George Johnson, | William P. Steere, | Baylies Bourne. |

1868.

President: George Johnson.

| Arlon Mowry, | Baylies Bourne, | Wm. Duane Aldrich, |
| Edward A. Brown, | William P. Steere, | Oscar A. Tobey. |

1869.

President: Arlon Mowry.

| Edward A. Brown, | William P. Steere, | George Johnson, |
| Baylies Bourne, | Oscar A. Tobey, | William H. Aldrich. |

1870.

President: Arlon Mowry.

| Edward A. Brown, | William P. Steere, | George Johnson, |
| Baylies Bourne, | Oscar A. Tobey, | William H. Aldrich. |

1871.

President: Arlon Mowry.

| Edward A. Brown, | William P. Steere, | George Johnson, |
| Baylies Bourne, | Oscar A. Tobey, | William H. Aldrich. |

TOWN TREASURERS.

John Sayles................	1731-50
Israel Wilkinson........	1750
Stephen Whipple..	1755
Capt. John Angell..................	1756-60
Stephen Whipple..	1761-9
William Buffum...........	1770-2
Arnold Paine.......................	1773-6
Uriah Alverson...........	1777-85
Stephen Brayton.......	1786-9I
Robert Harris. ...., ...	1792-1811
Isaac Wilkinson..................................	1812-39
Lewis Dexter.............................	1840-2
Stafford Mann....................................	1843
Samuel Clark..................	1844
Stafford Mann..	1845-9
Robert Harris..	1850-4
Henry Gooding..	1855-6
Thomas Moies......	1857
Reuel P. Smith..	1858-70

TOWN CLERKS.

Richard Sayles.....................	1731
Joseph Arnold, Jr.	1732
Daniel Jenckes...................................	1733-42
Joseph Arnold.......	1743-5
Thomas Sayles......	1746-54
Joseph Sayles....................	1755-9
John Sayles, Jr..	1756
Daniel Mowry, Jr...........	1760-1814
Samuel Mann...	1815-16
Thomas Mann.....................................	1817-39
George L. Barnes...	1840-2
Orrin Wright...	1843
George L. Barnes.................................	1844
Orrin Wright...	1845-49
Stafford Mann	1850-4
Samuel Clark.	1855-70

MODERATORS CHOSEN AT ANNUAL TOWN MEETINGS.

Jonathan Sprague, Jr	1731-2
Major William Smith	1733-5
Thomas Sayles	1736
Thomas Steere	1737
Thomas Sayles	1738
Thomas Steere	1739
Major William Smith	1740
Daniel Jenckes	1741
Thomas Sayles	1742-5
William Arnold	1746-8
Thomas Steere	1749-50
William Arnold	1751-2
William Jenckes	1753
William Arnold	1754
Thomas Steere	1755-7
Thomas Lapham	1758
Thomas Steere	1759-60
Thomas Lapham	1761
Thomas Steere	1762-4
Baulston Brayton	1765
Ezekiel Comstock	1766
Thomas Steere	1767
Ezekiel Comstock	1768
Thomas Steere	1769
John Sayles	1770-3
Ezekiel Comstock	1774-5
John Sayles	1776
Samuel Winsor	1777
Sylvanus Sayles	1778-80
Daniel Mowry, Jr.	1781
John Sayles	1782
Daniel Mowry, Jr	1783-4
Gideon Comstock	1785
Henry Jenckes	1786
Peleg Arnold	1787
Abraham Mathewson	1788
Sylvanus Sayles	1789
William Waterman	1790

Daniel Mowry	1791
John Sayles	1792
Sylvanus Sayles	1793
Daniel S. Mowry	1794
Sylvanus Sayles	1795
Peleg Arnold	1796
Sylvanus Sayles	1797
Peleg Arnold	1798
Sylvanus Sayles	1799
Ezekiel Comstock	1800
Peleg Arnold	1801-7
Duty Winsor	1808
Peleg Arnold	1809-16
Thomas Buffum	1817-19
George Chace	1820
Thomas Buffum	1821
Daniel Angell	1822
Thomas Buffum	1823-4
John Jenckes	1825
Arnold Spear	1826-30
George L. Barnes	1831-2
Arnold Spear	1833-6
Thomas Buffum	1837
Arnold Spear	1838
Louis Dexter	1839
John Jenckes	1840
David Daniels	1841
Daniel G. Harris	1842
David Daniels	1843
Thomas Mann	1844
David Daniels	1845
Gideon Bradford	1846-52
Daniel N. Paine	1853
Samuel S. Mallory	1854
Daniel N. Paine	1855
Samuel S. Mallory	1856
Sullivan Ballou	1857
Edward H. Sprague	1858
Spencer Mowry	1859
Bradbury C. Hill	1860
Spencer Mowry	1861

26

Daniel N. Paine.. 1862
Spencer Mowry... 1863-4
Bradbury C. Hill... 1865
Spencer Mowry... 1866
Bradbury C. Hill... 1867-8
Daniel N. Paine... 1869
Joseph M. Ross.. 1870

At a town meeting held on the sixteenth day of April, 1828, it was voted: That Henry S. Mansfield, John Jenckes, Thomas Buffum, George Smith, Mark Aldrich, David Wilkinson, Uriah Benedict, Samuel Hill, Jr., Daniel Jenckes, Lewis Dexter, Nicholas S. Winsor, Seth Mowry, Stephen Steere, Sessions Mowry, Luke Phillips, Caleb Farnum, Arnold Aldrich 2d, Abraham Winsor, Cyrus Arnold, Ezekiel Angell, Elisha Smith 3d, Arnold Bates, David Harris, John Dexter, and William Mowry 2d, be and they are hereby appointed a committee to district the town into school districts.

Voted: That all moneys appropriated for public schools shall be divided and appropriated as follows: one-half of the money to be equally divided among the schools, and the other half according to the number of scholars from four to twenty years old.

The School Committee was authorized to superintend the public schools and make the appropriations of money therefor.

SCHOOL COMMITTEES.

1828.

Barney Dodge,	William Buffum,	David Ide,
Manuel Shoules,	Luke Phillips,	Tyler Mowry,
Jonathan Andrews,	Joseph Mowry,	Sessions Mowry,
Asa Winsor,	Stephen Steere,	Elisha Smith,
Silas Smith,	Lewis Dexter,	Ezekiel Angell,
Daniel Jenckes,	Samuel Hill, Jr.,	John Jenckes.
	Daniel Jenckes 2d.	

1829.

Joseph Osborne,
Ephraim Coe,
Welcome Sayles,
Daniel Aldrich,
John S. Appleby,
Robert Harris,
David Wilkinson,

William Helme,
Asa Arnold,
William Mowry, Jr.,
William Harris,
Elisha Smith,
Ezekiel Angell,
George Smith,

Moses Aldrich,
Mark Aldrich,
Morton Mowry,
Asa Winsor,
Caleb Farnum,
Elisha Olney, Jr.,
Uriah Bennett.

1830.

George L. Barnes,
Samuel Bushee,
William Mowry, Jr.,
James Brown,
William Harris,
Eleazer Mowry,
David Wilkinson,

William Holmes,
Isaac Wilkinson,
Morton Mowry,
Asa M. Bartlett,
Elisha Smith,
Anthony Angell,
Israel Arnold, Jr.,

Rufus Tracy,
Welcome Sayles,
Rufus Arnold,
Reuben Mowry,
Caleb Farnum,
Joseph Briggs,
Uriah Bennett.

1831.

George S. Barnes,
Samuel Bushee,
William Mowry, Jr.,
James Brown,
Gideon Evans,
William Enches,
David Wilkinson,
Mark Aldrich,

William Holbrook,
Ezekiel Aldrich,
Morton Mowry,
Asa W. Ballou,
Elisha Smith,
Anthony Angell,
Henry S. Scott,
Samuel Clark,

Charles Smith,
William Sayles,
Lapham Jeffers,
Seth Mowry,
Winsor Farnum,
Joseph Briggs,
Uriah Bennett,
Samuel E. Gardiner.

1832.

Daniel Kendall,
George Aldrich 3d,
Ethan Harris,
Richard S. Scott,
Stephen Mowry,

Charles Smith,
Alden Coe,
Ransom J. Greene,
George W. Mowry,
Arnold Mowry,

Edward C. Cranston,
Otis Mowry,
David Wilbor,
William W. James,
Joseph Mowry 3d.

1833.

Stephen F. Brownell,
George Chace,
Ephraim Smith,
Alden Coe,
William Smith,
Wilder Holbrook,
Elisha Smith,

David Inman,
Richard Sayles,
Levi Mowry,
Seth Mowry,
Samuel Clark,
David Wilbor,
Nicholas Winsor.

Edward C. Cranston,
Uriah Bennett,
Moses Aldrich,
Otis Mowry,
Lyman Arnold,
Brown W. Sweet,

1834.

Stephen F. Brownell,	David Inman,	Edward C. Cranston,
George Chace,	Richard Sayles,	Uriah Benedict,
Ephraim Smith,	Levi Mowry,	Moses Aldrich,
Alden Coe,	Seth Mowry,	Otis Mowry,
William Smith,	Samuel Clark,	Lyman Arnold,
Wilder Holbrook,	David Wilbor,	Brown W. Sweet,
Elisha Smith,	Nicholas Winsor.	

1835.

Simeon Aldrich,	Charles A. Farnum,	Charles Moies,
Ephraim Smith,	Stephen Sheldon,	Arnold Spear,
Junior S. Latham,	Amasa Grant,	Ethan Harris,
Arnold Newell,	Samuel Clark,	Oliver Angell,
Jonathan Buxton,	Jesse Hutchinson,	Lemuel Alexander,
Augustus Wright,	Mowry Lapham,	Caleb Farnum,
John Fenner,	Nicholas S. Winsor,	Abraham Smith,
	Stephen Hopkins Smith.	

1836.

Simeon Aldrich,	Charles A. Farnum,	Charles Moies,
Ephraim Smith,	Stephen Sheldon,	Arnold Spear,
Junior S. Latham,	Amasa Grant,	Ethan Harris,
Arnold Newell,	Samuel Clark,	Oliver Angell,
Jonathan Buxton,	Jesse Hutchinson, Jr.,	Samuel Alexander,
Augustus Wright,	Mowry Lapham,	Caleb Farnum,
John Fenner,	Nicholas S. Winsor,	Abraham Smith,
	Stephen Hopkins Smith.	

1837.

Edward Hotchkiss,	Thomas Buffum,	Amos D. Lockwood,
Dennis Ballou,	Daniel Hendrick,	Elisha Mowry, Jr.,
Sterry Jenckes,	Ephraim Smith,	John Moies,
Jonathan Andrews,	Daniel Aldrich,	Robert W. Coe,
Gideon Mowry,	Ezekiel Angell,	Ephraim Sayles,
Henry S. Mansfield,	Smith Jenckes,	Simeon Aldrich, Jr.,
Fenner Mowry,	Caleb Farnum,	Asa Winsor,
Edward Evans,	Spencer Mowry,	Elisha Smith.

1838.
The Town Council.

1844.

Lewis Dexter,	John Foster,	Gideon Mowry,
Christopher W. Kelly,	Lyman Cooke,	Hiram Wilmarth,
	Ansel Holman.	

1845.

Gideon Bradford,	Metcalf Marsh,	Isaac Wilkinson,
Thomas Mann,	Stephen Benedict,	Richard Smith,
	Emor H. Smith.	

1846.

| Junior S. Mowry, | Charles Hyde, | Thomas D. Holmes. |

1847–8.

| Charles Hyde, | James Bushee, | Ahaz Mowry. |

1849.

| Isaac J. Burgess, | Samuel S. Mallory, | Thomas Steere. |

1850.

| Samuel S. Mallory, | Thomas Steere, | John P. Leonard. |

1851.

| Samuel S. Mallory, | John B. Tallman, | Howard W. King, |
| | William G. Arnold. | |

1852.

| Samuel S. Mallory, | Lysander Flagg, | James O. Whitney, |
| William G. Arnold, | Howard W. King. | |

1853.

| Samuel S. Mallory, | Howard W. King, | George C. Wilson. |

1854.

| Howard W. King, | Harvey Holmes, | George C. Wilson. |

1855.

| Howard W. King, | George C. Wilson, | Samuel S. Mallory, |

1856.

| Samuel S. Mallory, | Howard W. King, | Arlon Mowry. |

1857.

| Samuel S. Mallory, | Howard W. King, | Rev. Francis J. Warner. |

1858.

| John G. Richardson, | Howard W. King, | Rev. Francis J. Warner. |

1859.

John G. Richardson, Howard W. King,   William H. Seagraves.

1860.

John G. Richardson, Howard W. King,   Samuel O. Tabor,
                    Rev. Mowry Phillips.

1861.

John G. Richardson, Samuel O. Tabor,   Howard W. King,
                    Rev. Mowry Phillips.

1862.

John G. Richardson, Rev. Mowry Phillips, Samuel O. Tabor,
                    Thomas L. Angell.

1863.

Rev. Stewart Sheldon, Rev. Theodore Cook, Rev. Mowry Phillips,
                    Thomas L. Angell.

1864.

Lysander Flagg,   Augustus M. Aldrich, Marshall I. Mowry,
                    Rev. Richard Woodworth.

1865.

Rev. George H. Miner, Horace D. Paine,   George A. Kent,
                    Rev. Richard Woodworth.

1866.

Rev. George H. Miner, Horace D. Paine,   George A. Kent,
                    Rev. Richard Woodworth.

1867.

Edwin A. Buck,   Rev. R. Woodworth,   George A. Kent,
Rev. George W. Gill, Rev. Jas. E. Dockray, Ansel D. Nickerson.

1868.

Rev. Jas. E. Dockray, George A. Kent,   Marshall I. Mowry,
Ansel D. Nickerson, Rev. Robert Murray, Jr.,

1869.

Rev. R. Murray, Jr., George A. Kent,   Ansel D. Nickerson,
Webster Hazlewood, Marshall I. Mowry,   Samuel O. Tabor,
                    Rev. Charles E. Handy.

1870.

George A. Kent,   Rev. R. Murray, Jr., Rev. M. W. Burlingame,
Lysander Flagg,   Marshall I. Mowry,   Samuel O. Tabor.

At a town meeting, held August 25th, 1840, it was voted: That there shall be annually, hereafter, appointed a committee of three persons to examine those who may apply to be employed as teachers in this town, and if, in the opinion of one or more of said committee, such person is qualified as teacher, such member or members of said committee shall give such person a certificate to that effect; and that no person shall be entitled to receive any of the school money of this town who shall not have received such a certificate of qualification within six months previous to the time of such service as teacher; and, further, that the committee aforesaid be authorized and required to recommend such school books as they think most suitable to be used throughout the town; also, to visit the schools and make such suggestions for improvement as they may think proper.

EXAMINING COMMITTEE.

1840.

Amos D. Lockwood,　Nicholas S. Winsor,　Samuel S. Mallory.

In November, however, the number of said committee was ordered to be five.

James T. Harkness was chosen in place of Mr. Lockwood, who declined, and Thomas D. Holmes and David W. Aldrich were added.

1841.

Timothy A. Taylor.	Nicholas S. Winsor,	Samuel S. Mallory,
Thomas D. Holmes,	David W. Aldrich.	

1842.

Timothy A. Taylor,	Nicholas S. Winsor,	Thomas D. Holmes,
	Jenckes Mowry.	

1843.

Samuel S. Mallory,	Orin Wright,	Asa W. Ballou,
Metcalf Marsh,	James T. Harkness,	Jenckes Mowry,
John B. Tallman,	Jonathan Inman,	Boham P. Byrom,
	Bailey E. Borden.	

1844.

Timothy A. Taylor,	Nicholas S. Winsor,	Simon A. Sayles.
Thomas D. Holmes,	Charles E. Taylor.	

1845.

Gideon Bradford,	James T. Harkness,	George L. Barnes,
Samuel S. Mallory,	William Winsor.	

APPENDIX E.

LIST OF OFFICERS OF THE MILITIA BELONGING TO SMITHFIELD.

1775 to 1789.

1775. Elisha Mowry................Lieut.-Colonel, 2d Regiment.
   Andrew Waterman.................................Captain.
   Luke Arnold.................................... "
   Peleg Arnold.................................... "
   Joseph Jenckes................................. "
   Sylvanus Bucklin.........................Lieutenant.
1776. Andrew Waterman................................Captain.
   Elisha Mowry, Jr............Lieut.-Colonel, 2d Regiment.
   Thomas Jenckes..............................Captain.
   David Eddy.................................... "
   Nehemiah Smith................................ "
   Samuel Day..............................Lieutenant.
   Ebenezer Trask................................ "
   James Smith................................... "
   John Sayles, Jr...............................Colonel.
1777. Elisha Mowry, declined.......Lieut.-Colonel, 2d Regiment.
1778. John Angell.................. "   "
   Samuel Day...................................Captain.
   Ebenezer Trask................................ "
   Joseph Sprague................................ "
1779. John Angell................Lieut.-Colonel, 2d Regiment.
   Eber Angell.................................Captain.
   Ebenezer Trask................................ "
   Daniel Mowry 4th.............................. "
   Robert Bennett.........................Lieutenant.
   Simeon Ballou................................. "
   Benjamin Sheldon.............................. "
1780. John Angell................Lieut.-Colonel, 2d Regiment.
   William Aldrich.................Major, 2d Regiment.

	Eber Angell..... ....Captain.

Eber Angell..... ....Captain.
Ebenezer Trask.. .... "
Daniel Mowry, 4th... .... "
Robert Bennett.............................Lieutenant.
Simeon Ballou............................... "
Benjamin Sheldon.......................... "
1781. Peleg Arnold..... Lieut.-Colonel, Commandant 2d Battalion.
Job Mowry......................................Captain.
Benjamin Ballou............................... "
Ebenezer Trask .... "
Daniel Mowry 4th... .... "
Daniel Mowry 4th................ ....Major, 2d Regiment.
1784. Job Mowry........................ ....Captain.
Ebenezer Trask. .... "
George Streeter. .... "
Joel Aldrich. ....Lieutenant.
1785. Joel Aldrich..... ....Major, 2d Regiment.
William Aldrich..... ....Major, Senior Chaplain Regiment.
1786. Joel Aldrich........................Major, 2d Regiment.
1789. William Aldrich . ...Major, 2d Regiment.

LIST OF OFFICERS AND MEN WHO ENLISTED IN THE SERVICE
OF THE UNITED STATES, FROM SMITHFIELD, DURING
THE WAR OF THE REBELLION.

FIRST REGIMENT DETACHED MILITIA.

Thomas Steere, 1st Lieut.,
Henry C. Clark,
Daniel Sayles,
J. N. Woodward,
James Watson,
Job Arnold,
Nicholas B. Young,
George L. Keach,
Nelson Ballou,

Alexander F. Taylor,
William H. H. Cowden,
Albert E. Sholes,
William L. Eason,
G. M. Salisbury,
Edward W. Greene,
Thomas Young,
Benjamin O. Arnold,
Samuel Cash,

John E. Cowden,
Thomas Earle,
George Macomber,
Roderick Whipple,
Henry L. Cook,
Olney Marsh,
John H. Steere,
Ferdinand L. Watson,
Albert H. Abbott,
Arlon J. Follett,

George A. Earle,
James A. Gardiner,
Horace F. Allen,
Henry C. Mowry,
Barney J. Dodge,
Joseph N. Mason,
John S. Sanborn,
George D. Morris,
Zavier D. Fisher,
Hiram E. Taft.

SECOND REGIMENT R. I. VOLUNTEERS.

Sullivan Ballou, Major,
Charles E. Perkins, Captain,
Elisha Arnold, 1st Lieut.,
Stephen West, Jr., 1st Lieut.
Henry C. Cook, 2d Lieut,
Abraham Taylor,
Alney E. Nutting,
George T. Remington,
Henry Taft,
Leonard A. Clark,
Daniel G. Carpenter,
Stephen West, Jr.,
George E. Potter,
James Cromley,
David Cash,
Simeon Dean,
William H. Frazier,
George W. Fuller,
William Farrell,
Charles A. Godfrey,
John C. Hall,
Nathaniel G. Horton,
Robert L. Johnstone,
John Kelly,
Thomas McAlpin,
John Newell,
James Newell,
Patrick Island,
Israel Smith,

Marvin Smith,
James Fagan,
Almon Harris,
Albert E. Maker,
Giles C. Avery,
William Arnold,
James E. Boyce,
Hiram Bucklin,
Joseph C. Burnes,
Silas T. Watson,
Jenckes Patt.
J. P. Crandall,
Christopher A. Corey,
Edward O'Neal,
James F. Loomis,
James Martin,
Albert A. Mowry,
John J. Malone,
William W. Mowry,
Bernard McGarhen,
Joseph A. Phillips,
William H. Reed,
James F. Steere,
Charles W. Weeks,
William H. Augell,
Jencks Bartlett,
Charles E. Perkins,
Thomas O'Niell,
John F. O'Niell,

Edwin F. Steere, Serg't,
Lewis L. Sayles,
Silas G. Ballou,
William Hopkins,
George A. Pearce,
Michael Riley,
Albert W. White,
Preserved Angell,
Alfred I. Curtis,
Elisha Arnold,
Thomas Lewis,
Stephen Phetteplace,
John Chatman,
James K. King,
William C. Parker,
Charles E. Dunham,
Robert A. McCartney,
Simeon I. Staples,
George W. Kidder,
James W. Potter.

John H. Phillips,
George W. Harvey,
John Pasnett,
William Lomas,
George W. Olney,
Stephen West, Jr.,
William G. Reynolds,
Robert Robertson, Jr.,
Albert F. Smith,
James R. Pierce,
William Thomas,
Bradford Chamberlain,
Charles H. Hawkins,
George B. Hutchinson,
Lewis E. Angell,
James H. Brophy,
Patrick Carroll,
Joseph L. Haswell,
Wilson Aldrich,

THIRD REGIMENT R. I. HEAVY ARTILLERY.

Isaac Bishop,
Samuel Hyndam,
Irwin F. Mann,
Edwin Soule,
William H. Bateman,
John Baird,
Charles A. Baker,
Horatio N. Moon,
Edward P. Maguie,
Charles W. Nichols,
Thomas Phelan,
Hiram Phetteplace,
John Shuee,
Barton W. Saunders,
Erastus D. Whitcomb,
Olney Marsh,
John O'Connor,
Henry S. Jennison,
Daniel L. Arnold,

Samuel Kirk,
Arthur J. McAllen,
George F. Paine,
Moses A. Paine,
Hiram R. Parker,
John C. Pitts,
Charles R. Richardson,
Albert L. Ruby,
Edward Ryan,
Uriah Salley,
Lewis C. Sanborn,
Charles H. Smith,
Stephen H. Sanborn,
Levi Simmons,
Henry E. Williams,
Jashub Wing,
William H. H. Mowry,
Alonzo M. Fuller,
Stephen Rider,

Silas H. Appleby,
Alfred B. Brown,
Nelson M. Buffum,
William Davis,
Edward Black,
John H. Hodges,
Alonzo N. Fuller,
Sidney A. Fuller,
James B. Fuller,
Oscar F. Gifford,
Roger Hale,
Daniel B. Hill,
Albert Langley,
John McNally,
William McAllen,
George H. Smith,
James T. Warner,
Benjamin L. Sayles,
John O'Brien,
Edwin Mowry,
Arnold O. Messler,
Thomas Finley,
James Campbell,
John C. Oakley,
Elisha Mowry,
Tristram S. Dow,
Edward Black,

Samuel Carson,
George L. Burlingame,
John H. Bailey,
Daniel J. Stone,
Edward Eddy,
Benjamin Chace,
Edwin Salley,
Michael Glancy,
John Higgins,
James B. Hobron,
James D. Havens,
Abijah B. Havens,
William W. Hodges,
Edwin Joslin,
Henry C. Reynolds,
David Sanderson,
Christopher K. Wilbor,
Cornelius O'Sullivan,
James B. Hobson,
James O'Donnell,
Michael Cavanaugh,
Martin G. Thornton,
Andrew J. Alexander,
Henry J. Morris,
Daniel S. Olney,
Irwin F. Mann.
John Bierd,

FOURTH REGIMENT R. I. VOLUNTEERS.

Charles H. Green, Captain,
Geo. F. Crowingshield, 1st Lieut.
Charles H. Johnston, 1st Lieut.
William Sayer,
James Gamley,
James McCann,
Albert Burlingame,
Stephen Booth,
Moses Clemence,
Warren J. Cutting,
Isaac Charles, Jr.,
James Davis,

Erastus E. Lapham, Captain,
John E. Moies, 1st Lieut.
Edwin M. Smith,
Jacob Butterfield,
Henry W. Bullman,
Decatur M. Boyden,
Silas W. Cummings,
Cornelius Costigan,
Peter Curran,
George L. Carter,
James Craig,
William H. Carter,

Albert G. Hopkins,
Jeremiah Lan,
Martin Quigley,
William H. Staples,
Albert H. Staples,
Ephraim M. Staples,
John Shay,
Albert L. Steere,
Herbert N. Sweet,
John M. Parker,
Peter Stevens,
Joseph Kelley,
Robert Kennedy,
Patrick Kennedy,
Henry M. Potter,
John Reynolds,
Edwin Street,
John B. H. Eaglestone,
Charles H. Fuller,
William Farrell,
Samuel W. Farnum,
Samuel H. Gorton,
George B. Hill,
Joseph B. Moore,
Nelson T. Newman,
Charles A. Newell,
David Phetteplace,
John R. Case,
Edwin M. Smith,
Charles H. Briggs, Sr.,
John Barrington,
John E. Moies, Serg't.

Thomas Clancy,
Michael O. Day,
John Flood,
John N. Graves,
James Grinrod,
Sylvester Griffin,
Timothy Gracy,
James Hennaver,
John Hunt,
Andrew Kennedy,
George Clarence,
Walter B. Peck,
Solomon Butterfield,
Jabez Butterfield,
Henry Butterfield,
Edwin M. Smith,
Martin Sullivan,
Edwin Tyler,
George Wild,
George Smith,
Henry Wardell,
James Welch,
Fenner Latham,
John Beaumont,
Emor H. Bartlett,
William H. Nichols,
George Bassett,
Albert E. Sholes,
John A. Crowningshield,
Charles H. Briggs, Jr.,
Nathan Collins,

FIFTH REGIMENT R. I. HEAVY ARTILLERY.

John Aigan, Captain,
Dennis G. Ballou,
Jerry Sullivan,
Timothy Prior,
Ebenezer Balcolm,
Wilson D. Barnes,
Richard A. Brown, Corporal.

Richard Arnold,
James Flynn,
Charles Farrington,
Frank Fox,
Thomas Cooney,
Thomas Forbes,

SEVENTH REGIMENT R. I. VOLUNTEERS.

John Sullivan, 2d Lieut.
Joseph Coyle,
Peter Lamby,
Alonzo L. Jenckes,
Benjamin W. Keech,
Adams Murray,
Albert M. Smith,
George Buxton,
Joseph Battie,
Michael Rice,
Nelson Niles,
James S. Slater,
John A. Austin,
James J. Taylor,
Joseph J. D. Grayton,
Albert G. Durfee,
Dexter L. Brownell, 2d Lieut.,
Albert M. Smith,
George Buxton,
Joseph Battie,
Michael Rice,
Nelson Niles,
James S. Slater,
John Sullivan,
Mathew S. Belcher,
John Simpson,

John S. Belcher, 2d Lieut.
Stephen C. Jillson,
John F. Steere,
Henry W. Beebe,
John Brennan,
Charles F. Slocum,
Samuel Curtis,
George Fisher,
John Burke,
Francis W. Gardiner,
Edward A. Radikin,
Cyril P. Thornton,
John Simpson,
Hasson O. Whiting,
Horatio Steere,
William H. Smith,
Decatur M. Boyden,
Samuel Curtis,
George Fisher,
John Burke,
Francis W. Gardiner,
Edward A. Radikin,
Cyril P. Thornton,
John Sullivan, 2d Lieut.,
John A. Austin,
James J. Taylor,

NINTH REGIMENT R. I. VOLUNTEERS.

John McKinley, Captain,
Nathan Benton, 2d Lieut.,
Horatio Giles,
Andrew Crumley,
James H. Jolly,
Walter S. Sutcliff,
Fenner Colwell,
Trowbridge Smith,
Joseph Smith, Jr.,
William T. Brooks,

Isaac Place, Captain,
Israel Arnold, Jr.,
William Cory,
Thomas Crumley,
James O'Brien,
Richard J. Whittle,
George W. Haradon,
George H. Johnson,
Byron S. Thompson,
David Dines,

James Jacques,
Henry E. Baker,
Gilbert A. Thompson,
Cyrus Bennett,
Jacob Butterfield,
Willard D. Colwell,
William F. Fuller,
John Gallagher,
Alexander Henderson,
Walter Matthew,
Thomas Pryor,
Joseph Sedgwick,
James Sullivan,
Thomas B. Spooner,
Enoch Spencer,
Alexander Tongue,
Joseph Wilmarth,
George Wilson,
Moses Brown,
Stephen P. Steere,
Thomas Britton,
Charles Bowers,
Sylvanus Holbrook, Jr.,
Arnold Jennerson,
John Niles,
Otis W. Smith,
Jarvis Smith,
John Westgate,
A. Sayles Clark,
Jenckes Bartlett,
Edwin Carter,
John H. Durgin,
Albert Hudson,
Thomas Lewis,
George S. Potter,
Henry C. Sayles,
John Swindler,
Joseph Wheelock,
George P. Grant,
William C. Benedict,
David E. Cash,
Henry Crocker,

Martin G. Cushman,
Samuel Preston,
Moses A. Aldrich,
Henry Bennett,
George W. Buxton,
George B. Evans,
Frederick C. Gove,
Thomas Hughes,
Martin G. Lyons,
William F. Miller,
John Regan,
Robert Sanford,
John Sullivan,
Justin Stevens,
Winfield S. Thompson,
Charles F. Taft,
Thomas D. Wilson,
Edward F. Steere,
John E. Whipple,
Daniel W. Brayton,
George Britton,
John Burns,
Thomas L. Hopkins,
Jesse D. Keach,
George Smith,
Thomas Smith,
William T. Smith,
James A. Sweet,
Charles W. Bradford,
Asa Bennett,
Foster W. Clark,
Caleb H. Freeman,
George J. Hendrick,
Charles A. Pierce,
Thomas Riley,
Marcus L. Sweet,
Isaac S. Tanner,
Edmund Crocker,
Alanson P. Wood,
Robert E. Curran,
Warren F. Cook,
Byron E. Daggett,

Bemjamin A. Dennis,
James H. Fairbanks,
Edward A. Patt,
Stephen A. Peck,
Anthony G. Wood,
Charles D. Wood.

David L. Fales,
Joseph B. Gooding,
William G. Thurber,
John E. Whiting,
Henry H. Welden,

TENTH REGIMENT R. I. VOLUNTEERS.

Samuel H. Hopkins,
Arnold J. Paine,
Albert W. Sprague,

Alden Paine,
Stephen Phetteplace,
George H. Tyler.

ELEVENTH REGIMENT R. I. VOLUNTEERS.

Thomas Moies, 1st Lieut.,
Edmund F. Crocker,
George Cushman,
George W. Gooding,
Nathan L. Baggs,
Ansel Baxter,
Henry T. Braman,
Jasper Caler,
Patrick Cavanaugh,
Nicholas P. Clark,
James Coyle,
Thomas Dolan,
William F. Elsbree,
Henry A. Follett,
Theodore C. Fuller,
Charles C. Holland,
William Horton,
Peter Knoth,
Barney Mahan,
Gilbert Mann,
Charles P. Moies,
John McCormick,
John McCreighton,
Ansel D. Nickerson,
Levi C. Phillips,
David N. Rogers,
Daniel E. Verry,

Joseph W. Grosvenor, Ass't Surg,
James N. Woodward,
David L. Fales,
Orman L. Patt,
George G. Bennett,
Daniel Bryce,
Edward A. Browne,
James D. Carpenter,
Michael Cassiday,
Warren F. Cook,
James Curran,
Andrew J. Dexter,
J. Henry Fales,
William B. Follett,
Charles E. Griffin,
Joseph E. Hood,
Michael Killeran,
Thomas S. Lindsay,
Nathan P. Maker,
Barney McNally,
Edward McCormick,
James Mulhaven,
John J. Niell,
William O'Donnell,
Thomas Rice,
Michael Trainor,
Philip Vickerey,

Thomas S. White,
Joseph W. Guild,
John A. Rupert,
Joseph S. Bunker,
Henry S. Sharpe,
George Lovely,
William C. White,

Charles H. Wilmarth,
Elisha Place,
Adin Patt,
Andrew Campbell,
John S. Graham,
David S. Linch,
Daniel R. Ballou,

TWELFTH REGIMENT R. I. VOLUNTEERS.

Richard A. Briggs, 1st Lieut.,
William Ackinson,
James Ackinson,
Joseph W. Preston,
William Reddy,
Joseph Wilmarth,
Oren Mowry,
George E. Macomber,
Edwin P. Williams,
Benajah S. Allen,
James Phetteplace,
Mowry C. Colwell,
Collins V. Keith,
Shadrack O. Mowry,
John H. White,

Henry Britton,
William A. Andrews,
George E. Brown,
Otis P. Cleveland,
William H. Greene,
James L. Burlingame,
John E. Thornton,
Charles J. Sweet,
Lewis G. Arnold, Jr.,
Amasa Phetteplace,
Horace W. Cook,
Thomas M. Green,
William H. Latham,
Daniel Pelky,
George A. Britton.

FOURTEENTH REGIMENT HEAVY ARTILLERY.

George A. Pearce, 1st Lieut.,   Daniel Carver.

FIRST REGIMENT R. I. LIGHT ARTILLERY.

William H. Walcott,
Henry F. Clark,
Edward Morrisey,
Thomas P. Steere,
Joseph A. Cole,
Albert E. Hendrick,
George W. Nichols,
Charles W. Hudson,
George A. Perry,
Patrick Sullivan,
Lewis L. Sayles,

William Arnold,
Patrick Larkin,
Joseph S. Nichols,
John Appleby Thornton,
John Eatock,
John B. Mowry,
Charles O. Dyer,
Charles E. Mathewson,
James Quigley,
Benjamin Snell,
Elisha D. Thayer,

28

Olney Arnold,
Daniel W. Elliott,
William H. Cartwright,
William H. Steere,
Esek S. Owen,
Michael Barry,
Benjamin Carter,
Michael Murray,
Otis P. Snell,
Barney Cassidy,
Wm. H. Phinney,
Henry J. White,
Jacob Waldberger,
John Gray,
Daniel Cæsar,

Royal W. Ceaser,
Jesse D. Keach,
Thomas Phinney,
Albert V. Walker,
Joy G. Bellows,
Gilbert Carman,
Thomas J. Loftus,
William H. Stone,
Aaron Schanck,
Wm. H. C. Smith,
Philip, A. Dexter,
Charles W. Warren,
Robert Sheridan,
Patrick Cornell,
Thomas Donnelly.

TENTH R. I. LIGHT BATTERY.

William Landigan,
John Stewart,

Joseph McClellan,
Patrick Gleason.

FIRST REGIMENT R. I. CAVALRY.

John Winsor,
Jesse W. Angell,
Ethan S. Brown,
William B. Ford,
James Winterbottom,
Marcus W. Sweet,

Daniel A. Smith,
William H. Latham,
Allen T. Brown,
John H. Steere,
George W. Harris,
William A. Tucker,

Thomas Pinkerton.

SECOND REGIMENT R. I. CAVALRY.

Henry J. Whittaker, 1st Lieut.
Martin C. Cushman,
Frederick Campbell,
Thomas Prior,
Francis Reynolds,
Aris Bourgen,

Horace D. Allen,
Alexander Brenno,
Alexander Campbell,
William J. Perry,
Roswell Saltonstall,
Thomas Crumley,

George Crumley.

THIRD REGIMENT R. I. CAVALRY.

Lyman L. Swan, Asst. Surg.,
Nathan L. Boggs,
Peter Gilroy,
Robert M. Pollard,
Wilson D. Mundy,
Alexander Simpson,
George H. Howard,
Henry Mowry,
Thomas Smith,
William Rankin,

John B. Batcheller,
Nicholas B. Gardner,
Augustus Binford,
Amos Perry,
Anslem Sansany,
Jonathan M. Boss,
Thomas R. Hawkins,
James McCabe,
George Spaulding,
Edward S. Tyler.

SEVENTH SQUADRON R. I. CAVALRY.

Christopher Vaughan, Captain,
George A. Smith,
Daniel H. Goff,
Antoine Allen,
Timothy Collins,
John Higgins,
James McWilliams,
James Sullivan,
John Taylor,
Caleb Watson,
Henry B. Jennison,
John McGovern,
Daniel Pierce,

John Angell, 1st Lieut.
Thomas Dwyer,
Jeremiah Amidon,
James Crofter,
Alexander Henderson,
Thomas Harper,
James Ryder,
Ralph Street,
James P. White,
Wilson S. Mowry,
Martin Winsor,
Benjamin T. Reynolds,
Edward Morrisey.

FIFTEENTH REGIMENT MASSACHUSETTS VOLUNTEERS.

James Shay,

Martin Winsor.

UNITED STATES CHASSEURS.

George Harris,

Olney Clark.

FOURTEENTH REGIMENT U. S. INFANTRY.

George Watson.

TWENTY-FOURTH REGIMENT MASSACHUSETTS VOLUNTEERS.

John Payson,

George W. Wallace.

IN OTHER MASSACHUSETTS REGIMENTS.

Lully B. Mowry,   Elisha Steere.

POPULATION OF SMITHFIELD.

1731	450
1755	1,921
1774	2,888
1776	2,781
1782	2,217
1790	3,171
1800	3,120
1810	3,828
1820	4,678
1830	6,857
1840	9,534
1850	11,500
1860	13,283
1865	12,315

INDEX.

CHAPTER I.

CHAPTER II.

29

CHAPTER III.

APPENDIX A.

APPENDIX B.

Assistants and Senators in the General Assembly, from the town of Smithfield, from 1731 to 1798:

APPENDIX C.

Deputies and Representatives in the General Assembly:

APPENDIX D..

APPENDIX E.

List of officers and men who enlisted in the service of the United States from Smithfield during the war of the rebellion:

INDEX

HILL, 99 106 162 164 181 191
201 202 212 213 Bradbury
C 67 83 84 105 154 Daniel
102 David 100 George 60
100 102 Judge 99 Mr 105
106 Phillips 67 Samuel 106
Samuel Jr 99 106
HINES, Philemon 53
HOBRON, 212
HOBSON, 212
HODGES, 212
HOIGHT, Jonathan 44
HOLBROOK, 194 203 204 215
HOLLAND, 216 C C 127
HOLMAN, 180 181 195 205
Ansel 94
HOLMES, 203 205 207
Thomas D 67 69
HOLT, 181 George W 83
HOOD, 216
HOPKINS, 211 213 215 216
Jonathan 53 Stephen 36
HORTON, 196 210 216
HOTCHKISS, 204
HOWARD, 219
HOWELL, David 56
HUDSON, 215 217
HUGHES, 215
HUNT, 213
HUTCHINSON, 204 211
HYDE, 205
HYNDAM, 211
IDE, 202 David 64 E 67
INCHES, Thomas 30
INDIAN, Assotemewit 6
Cannannicus 6 Canonicus
5 Canuaunicus 6 Meaun-
tonomi 6 Miantonomi 5 6
Seatash 6

INGRAHAM, Dwight 117 H N
115 118 Jabal 117
INMAN, 203 204 207
IRONS, 181 197 Dexter 65
Samuel 30
ISLAND, 210
JACKSON, Charles 105
JACQUES, 215
JAMES, 203 II King Of Eng-
land 18
JEFFERS, 203
JEFFRIES, David 33
JENCKES, 162 165 166 171
173 174 184-192 194 199-
202 204 208 214 Adam 60
Amos T 61 Benjamin 58
Christopher 28 Daniel 58
67 Daniel C 67 David 58
George 58 John 28 46 51
60 66 67 70 John II 62
John Jr 58 60 Joseph 34
Joshua 45 60 Nicholas 58
60 Oliver 59 Sterry 66
Susannah 62 Thomas 37
Thomas A 101 William 60
Wm 28
JENCKS, 165 166 180 Joseph
33 34
JENKES, Dr 27
JENKINS, 101 Anna 100 Wil-
liam 100 Wm 116
JENKS, 114 195 Alvin 117
120 Alvin F 113 Andrew
117 Benjamin 113 David
116 117 George 116 117
George F 115 117 118
Gideon 113 114 Joseph
110 Moses 114 Stephen
114-116 118 Stephen A

www.ingramcontent.com/pod-product-compliance
Lightning Source LLC
Chambersburg PA
CBHW061722270326
41928CB00011B/2083